CALIFORNIA GOLD

STORY OF THE
RUSH TO RICHES

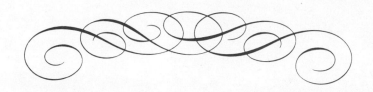

A MINI-HISTORY
BY PHYLLIS AND LOU ZAUNER

Other Zanel Publications mini-histories:

A GRAND ADVENTURE

Gold changed the destiny of a nation.

Its accidental discovery in 1848 by a moody, not-too-bright carpenter set off the most frenzied gold rush in the history of the world, and the greatest mass migration of human beings ever known. It turned California - until then a sparsely populated, largely unknown region - into a household word throughout the world.

Before 1848, California was a sleepy, languid land. The Mexicans (and their predecessors, the Spanish) settled the coastal lands on vast tracts donated to them by the Mexican government, and turned it into a delightful playground. No one worked hard; the men practiced horsemanship, the women embroidered. The boring chores of life were relegated to servants.

Inland California, even wilder, was the domain of Indians...and later the domicile of a few settlers who had been granted estates by the Mexican government. Captain John Sutter was the most notable.

As 1848 opened, the United States had just wrested this charming, lonely land from Mexico after a brief skirmish or two, mainly because there was too much of it for the Mexicans to hang onto.

For that matter, there was no assurance the United States would fare better controlling such a faraway settlement. California was then, in truth, a remote island, cut off from the civilized world of the East by 1,800 miles of broiling desert and impassable mountains. By sea, it was 18,000 miles distant, via Cape Horn.

This, then, was the setting on a crisp, cold January morning when an ordinary carpenter, James Marshall, went down to the river to look at the progress of construction on a mill he was building for John Sutter.

"One morning in January - it was a clear, cold morning, I shall never forget that morning - as I was taking my usual walk along the race after shutting off the water, my eye was caught with the glimpse of something shining in the bottom of the ditch. There was about a foot of water running then. I reached my hand down and picked it up. It made my heart thump, for I was certain it was gold."

Marshall's cataclysmic discovery failed to ignite any widespread enthusiasm for several months. A San Francisco newspaper gave it four sentences on a back page; few readers took the news seriously. In fact, editors themselves called it a hoax.

The man who turned the world's blindness to 20-20 vision was Sam Brannan, a shrewd entrepreneur who (by fortuitous chance!) owned a general store near the gold discovery site. Having satisfied himself that there was, indeed, gold for the picking, he gathered up a small bottle of nuggets at Coloma, headed for San Francisco, and rode up and down Montgomery Street booming, "Gold! Gold from the American River!"

The effect of Brannan's enthusiastic announcement on San Francisco was electrifying. Virtually the entire population (450) packed off to the hills, hysterical with gold lust. According to a contemporary account, "The blacksmith dropped his hammer, the carpenter his plane, the mason his trowel, the farmer his sickle, the baker his loaf, and the tapster his bottle. All were off for the mines, some on carts, some on crutches, one even went in a litter."

The rush of 1848 was strictly local. Something like a quarter-million dollars in gold was pried from California before the winter rains set in. Except for a large group that wandered north from Sonora, Mexico, and a few who drifted in from Oregon Territory, the miners came almost entirely from within California.

When word finally reached the East Coast, most Americans were sure the reports were exaggerated, until President Polk informed Congress: "The accounts of the abundance of gold in that territory are of such an extraordinary character as would scarcely command belief."

It was like an official sanction. An entire nation became delirious with gold fever. As if by command, literally thousands upon thousands dropped everything and headed for California.

The first wave to leave for the land of golden promise engaged passage on whatever ships were available, and set off on a tedious, sometimes harrowing voyage around Cape Horn that would take six months to reach San Francisco. Some chose the shorter, though far more dangerous, sea route via Panama. In Panama they put in at the Gulf port of Chagres; from there it was by muleback across the Isthmus to Panama City, where the wait for another ship heading up the coast might take months. Some didn't make it; they caught yellow fever before they caught the boat.

The hardest, but most popular, route to California was overland, across trackless plains, rugged mountains, and waterless deserts. It was a trek that couldn't be undertaken until spring, when forage grass was tall enough to sustain pack animals.

The hazards were many, and the multitudes who tried it were mostly ill-prepared. Consequently, their hardships and deprivations were some of the most harrowing in western folklore. Still they went.

The stampede was on, like some pestilential wave. California's charming pastoral life was smashed forever.

GOLD RUSH OF '48

So plentiful was gold that first summer that the boys treated it recklessly, as though the supply would have no end.

For centuries, the precious metal had been accumulating. Each spring the melting snows would trickle down the Sierras, depositing another crop of gold flecks and nuggets in crevices or in calm waters along the foothills. Happy miners literally stumbled over chunks of gold by sheer accident.

A man named McKnight chased a runaway cow, stubbed his toe on an outcropping of quartz, and sure enough, there was a fortune. A German struck a three-ounce nugget while digging a hole for a tent pole. Three Frenchmen uprooted a tree stump from the middle of the Coloma road and dug $5,000 in gold from the hole. A prospector staked out his mule for the night; when he pulled the stake in the morning the hole was gleaming with gold.

Such stories percolated across the western landscape and inflamed an already gold-hungry populace. The tales, however flamboyant, wore the trappings of truth, naming names and places.

And so the whole population of California simply transferred to the foothills. So assured were the men of an easy fortune that they sometimes arrived on the scene with nothing but a jack knife. Everyone was an amateur, none had ever mined, but all expected to get rich overnight. Some tried to be not too greedy. One newcomer declared, "If I don't pick up more than a hatful of gold a day, I shall be perfectly satisfied."

It was a remarkable phenomenon that in the midst of such easy wealth, the mines were practically free of crime that first year. A shovel or pick lying in a hole was the accepted sign of ownership. No one thought of jumping the claim. Belongings left in camp were unmolested; even bottles or bags of gold were left unguarded. It was simpler to gather gold than to steal it.

Poker was the favored entertainment of miners, and one eyewitness reported a game where the pot had grown so high that one player needed more dust to see the last raise. Putting his pile to one side, he calmly remarked to a companion, "Here, Jim, watch my pile until I go out and dig enough to call him."

The few cases of crime that came up were dealt with by "letting the punishment fit the crime." One rascal who stole a sack of gold and stashed it away, hastily repented after he was tied to a tree near a creek, his back laid bare to the bloodthirsty mosquitoes.

But if gold was free for the picking, there was always someone around who felt free to pick his share of the pickings -- the camp merchant.

"Fleecing the Golden Fleecers" became a lively and profitable business. In Sacramento, gateway to the treasure, men like Collis Huntington and Sam Brannan were waxing wealthy supplying the bare necessities of mining: shovels, picks and wash pans at a 1500 per cent mark-up. Within three months of the first wave of digging, Colonel Mason reported that Brannan & Company "had received in payment for goods $36,000 worth of gold from the 1st of May to the 10th of July."

When the interminable winter rains descended on the foothills, most of the Forty-Eighters were driven downhill to Sacramento or back to their families to wait for the spring melting of Sierra snow. But some stayed near their claims, puttering at mining, soaked to the skin much of the time. Some miners claimed the rain fell harder inside the cabins than it did outside.

"The rainy season set in. It rained three days, and I knew I had to get to San Francisco. What I was making in the mines was a mere nothing compared to what I had at stake there. But I never left a place with more regret, as hard as the fare was. We were interested every day in the work for gold, and did not know when we might make a rich strike.

"My last day, the rain notwithstanding, a companion and myself went out to dig for a couple of hours. When we returned we had $25 worth. That was the last of my mining. I sold my pistol and blankets for an ounce each, $16. The next morning I started for Sacramento afoot."   - Daniel Knower

In the spring of 1849, following President Polk's State-of-the-Union message, the dam of ignorance that had held the rest of the country back, broke loose. Gold fever, until then a local outbreak in a remote and almost unheard of place, all at once became an international epidemic. In 1849 more than a hundred thousand people poured into California. Gold mania swept the East, jumped the Atlantic to England, invaded Germany and France. Those who came by ship docked in San Francisco, turning the small hamlet into a virtual boomtown. Tents and makeshift housing covered the hills. Ships clogged the harbor, many abandoned by their crews for the diggings. Mud in the streets got so deep that men drowned in it.

Sacramento, a sort of warehouse and gathering point for the mining district, changed almost overnight from a muslin-and-canvas village of 120 population, to a full-blown city. Two hundred houses went up that first spring.

And up and down the foothills, instant towns sprang up like toadstools on a wet morning, christened with raffish names that tickled the miners' fancy - Rich Bar, Gomorrah, Delirium Tremens, Humbug, Jackass Hill, You Bet, or Bed Bug. Most vanished overnight if the gold petered out. All were tinderboxes, just a spark away from obliteration on a boisterous Saturday night.

He got outfitted with everything a miner should need, had his picture taken in a Minnesota studio...but never left home.

The 'Age of Innocence' ended with the Forty-Eighters. Life was sometimes raw. All the vices money could buy surfaced. Men drank and gambled in excess. They spend their dust recklessly. If they had worked hard for it, they felt they owed themselves a treat. If it came easy, they felt they could always get more. Fortunes were made and lost, sometimes all in one day. When a strike was made and gold was flowing freely, the camp store supplied men with sardines, oysters, French champagne. For men down on their luck, rancid bacon and beans sufficed.

For all who struck it rich, there were thousands who hunkered ankle-deep in cold mountain streams rotating a pan, or shovelled a ton of gravel a day into a long tom, eking out a bare existence.

Still and all, it was a life of excitement, win or lose. The wild ways of the West were a release from the drudgery of everyday life they had known back home; an escape from the ordinary. And for some, their toil at rockers and long toms was better than the creditors, mothers-in-law and hard-bitten employers they had left behind.

The California Gold Rush was an extraordinary episode in American history, a story of courage and heroism, of cowardice and selfishness. It lasted barely a decade. The brash young men who were a part of it, whose search for gold settled a remote land in months instead of years, had a grand, gaudy adventure they never forgot.

In spite of the misery of loneliness, hardship, and backbreaking work - and sometimes broken dreams - they had "seen the elephant."

"Panning is a very curious and mysterious operation," one of the new miners wrote home. *"I did as I was told, whirling and dipping with all my might. There was nothing in the appearance of the earth to distinguish it from what I had seen a thousand times at home. Yet this was the earth I had come twenty thousand miles to seek, and in that earth there lurked, so I was told, grains of gold."*

The phrase *"seeing the elephant,"* came to mean the excitement of the lure of California gold. It is said to have originated in a story about a farmer who had heard of elephants but had never seen one. When a circus came to a nearby town, he loaded his wagon with eggs and vegetables and started for the market, determined to see a circus elephant. On the way he met the circus parade, led by the elephant. The farmer was enchanted, but his horses were terrified. They bucked, pitched, overturned the wagon and ran away, scattering eggs and bruised vegetables over the countryside. *"I don't give a hang,"* said the farmer, *"I have seen the elephant."*

HO FOR CALIFORNIA!

Not until 1848 drew to a close did the eastern seaboard awake to the golden opportunity on the far side of the continent.

By that November the electrifying possibilities for becoming rich had fired everyone's imagination, and gold mania became a national fever. Horace Greeley's *New York Tribune* announced, "We are on the brink of the Age of Gold!" His estimate of the gold available ran to "at least one thousand millions of dollars."

And so the surge to California began. It sent thousands of otherwise sensible and sober men journeying desperately across deserts and trackless plains, through tropical swamps, and into gales at sea -- "off to Californy."

Some simply hitched up their farm wagons and started walking west, but most joined in companies organized for the long transcontinental trail. Others used faster but more complicated routes across the Isthmus of Panama. Most of those who lived on the east coast made the 13,000-mile voyage all the way around South America.

But no matter which way they went, it was a journey fraught with perils.

THE OVERLAND ROUTE

The marshalling point was the Missouri River, and by May it was crowded with eager adventurers waiting for winter to end. The time of departure had to be carefully calculated. Those who started too early risked swollen streams and scant forage grass. A late summer start could mean snow blocking mountain passes.

It was a busy scene, with constant buying and swapping of oxen, horses and mules. Traders were there with strings of Mexican mules, claimed to be more reliable in arid, stony, mountainous country than the larger Missouri mules. Oxen were favored, too; they were slow but patient.

Mostly the forty-niners overpacked. Later, on the trail, wagon wheels got stuck in mud and deep sand, so that the routes westward were littered with stoves and trunks and fancy mining machines. Facing desert stretches, all room was needed for water storage.

Wagon trains followed three major westward routes, but most of them (at least 22,500 in 1849) took the familiar emigrant trail -- from the Missouri to the Platte and Sweetwater rivers, around Salt Lake, across the inhospitable Great Basin desert, to the Sierra, last barrier to California.

Along the rivers, the men found few problems (and sometimes glorious vistas). Indians gave the men a fright on first encounter -- "Frank stole my pistols," recorded one diarist, "and drank a pint of whisky to keep his courage up." But it ended in a trading session.

A far worse hazard was cholera, at that time a raging epidemic along the rivers. Victims were buried in unmarked graves. No one knew how to avoid getting it, but "Dr. Zoril's cure-all medicine" was favored by some. And some put their trust in a lump of asafetida worn around the neck "to ward off spasms."

After passing over the Continental Divide, the forty-niners came to the first desert -- a 400-mile stretch with no river valleys to open the way, until they reached a bluff overlooking the Green River. "Dusty sage bushes, and hosts of dead oxen," the diarist recorded. "Before we reached the river, cattle became aware we were nearing water and showed signs of great impatience." He added, "It was a grand sight." The cattle, released from the yoke, went tumbling down the steep embankment to wallow in the water.

The most excruciating desert, though was the 40-mile wasteland that extended from the place the Humboldt River simply disappears in sand, to the Carson River at the foot of the Sierra. "The alkali dust is suffocating, irritating our throats. Clouds of it blind us. Mirages tantalize us. Any water found is unfit to use. Animals are overcome by heat and exhaustion and have to be abandoned."

After that, the argonauts faced the climb over the Sierra -- dangerous, exhausting and painfully slow. Sometimes the wagons had to be unloaded, and men and mules packed everything on their backs. To lower wagons on steep grades, willows were stuffed between wheel

spokes, and men pulled on lines to hold the wagon from making a disastrous descent. Sometimes mules fell over cliffs and wagons were wrecked.

The trip from Missouri took a hundred days. And few of them were filled with joy.

THE VOYAGE AROUND CAPE HORN

Gold seekers from eastern shores were used to the idea of ocean travel so it was natural to think of getting to the gold fields by ship.

In the beginning, the route most favored was south to the tip of South America, around Cape Horn, and up the Pacific, a trip that took four to eight months.

There were some advantages. For one, it could be undertaken in winter. Also, more baggage could be taken.

Nevertheless, passengers got heartily sick of the sea, the tedium of endless days, of seasickness, and the food. Those who weren't too seasick to eat complained that "the salt pork was rusty, the dried beef rotten, and there were two bugs for every bean." Unless the passenger thought to bring his own fresh fruit, scurvy was a serious threat. Water stored for months on end in the ship's vats developed a remarkably foul taste. And occasionally, by the end of the voyage, food simply ran out, though live hogs were brought along to be slaughtered aboard.

For some, though, the voyage had its exotic moments. The city of Rio de Janiero charmed them. They trooped by the palace, toured the cathedral, tasted bananas ("you just eat the core, the skin is bitter").

Far different was the struggle around the Horn. Waves crashed over the bow, sending water through the hatches and leaky decks to the passenger holds below. Pitching and rolling were constant. Some passengers were simply lost overboard, some lashed themselves to their berths. Now and then the ship would tremble as though hit by an iceberg. So wild were the gales that raked the Cape that a schooner could be lifted from the water and slammed ashore, a prospect that prompted one passenger to comment, "These times have harmonized our minds on one point, some other way to California is preferable."

Still, the Cape Horn route was the safest path to California in 1849. A few died of scurvy, a few were swept overboard, and exploding boilers were occasionally a danger. But the toll was nothing like the overland trail to gold.

CROSSING THE PANAMA ISTHMUS

The most expensive route, and in some respects the most perilous, was through the Panama Isthmus. Travelers had to arrange passage on two

ships on two oceans, and in between they were at the mercy of natives who quickly caught on to the value of inflated prices.

After sailing down the Atlantic, passengers disembarked at the mouth of the Chagres River, a fever-ridden region of swamps infested with alligators, poisonous plants, quicksand, and clouds of mosquitoes. From there they had to make their way 75 miles across to the Pacific side, to the broken-down city of Panama City.

The first 50-mile leg was made in long dugout canoes called bungos, which were paddled or poled by natives who overcame fatigue with frequent siestas, occasionally stoking themselves with rum.

The air was heavy and the heat unbearably oppressive, but passengers amused themselves with drinking brandy and trying out their new firearms on iguanas and other wildlife in the jungles.

The second leg of the overland journey was by muleback or afoot, slogging through jungles alive with insects and snakes. Many passengers were already suffering the aches and fevers of cholera and malaria. Others were sure to die of yellow fever.

By the time the 24-mile trip ended, everyone was bone-weary, bone-chilled after sundown, and drenched in sweat.

Arriving in Panama City, a decaying town of shacks and ruined buildings, they were likely to find no ships available for the Panama-California journey. Hotels were almost non-existent. Pioneer Hiram Pierce and his company waited 35 days before they could get passage in any kind of vessel. Covered with mosquito bites, they shook with chills, and burned with fever. When a ship finally arrived, Pierce recorded, "it was overcrowded and wretched dirty."

In general, the few ships plying the Panama-California run were wholly inadequate for the horde of gold seekers. Many sailed for San Francisco and never returned. Thus the crowd of stranded California-bound adventurers multiplied at a staggering rate.

THE GOLDEN LAND

One way or another -- through the Isthmus, around the Horn, or across the plains -- it was an undertaking to be entered upon in grim earnest, as those knew well who at length arrived in the gold fields. Not one but planned to go home as soon as he had made his pile.

Not a one knew they were tomorrow's Californians, that they would build a new state, a new civilization, or that a third of them would never return to their former homes again.

JOHN SUTTER'S GRANDIOSE DREAM

Mexican California might have slept undisturbed for decades more, save for one man: John Sutter. Urbane and polished, he was one of the West's most remarkable pioneers.

It was his ambitious plan to persuade the Mexican government to grant him land in the uninhabited inland valley so he could build himself an empire, a place he could live in genteel aristrocacy.

For Governor Alvarado, the 30-year-old Mexican in charge of ruling California, it was the heaven-sent answer to his problems with unruly Indians and encroaching trappers from the United States. He made Sutter a Mexican citizen and granted him 76 square miles.

And so in 1839 Sutter set out across the Bay and the delta waters with three boats and a crew of 13 into a wilderness populated only by Indians and mosquitoes. He carried provisions, agricultural implements and weapons as he searched out a route through the delta.

"It took me eight days to find the Sacramento River, as it is very easy to pass by," he recorded in his diary.

The land Sutter chose was a gently rising knoll well back from the river. The first task was to construct an adobe building before the winter rains set in. Nearly 40 feet long, it became the nucleus of Sutter's Fort, one of the most famous of all western frontier outposts.

With the help of Indians, he constructed a wall around it 18 feet thick, a headquarters building, and a long line of workshops. He laid a rough road to the river so he could ship goods to San Francisco. By the following summer he had planted crops and acquired some cattle and horses on credit from a rancher on the Carquinez Strait.

Occasionally he had visitors. In 1841 John Bidwell and a party of 30 came over the Sierra. "Nearly everybody who came to California," Bidwell wrote, "made it a point to reach Sutter's Fort. Sutter was one of the most hospitable of men. Everyone was welcome. One man or a hundred, it was all the same."

In time Sutter realized the need for a sawmill, so he sent James Marshall to build it on a stream in the foothills 30 miles away.

And it was here that the course of western history changed. While dredging out the tailrace of the mill, Marshall discovered gold nuggets in fine silt that had washed over the rocks.

The discovery by no means precipitated an instant gold rush. In fact, Marshall waited several days before making a trip to Sacramento to tell Sutter the news.

After Sutter had seen the gold, he took out an old encyclopedia to find the test for gold, went to the apothecary shop in the fort and got aqua fortis to test it. It was, indeed, gold.

Excited as he was, it wasn't hard to see what could happen to his various enterprises once word got out. The two men agreed to keep the matter quiet until the sawmill was finished.

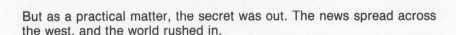

But as a practical matter, the secret was out. The news spread across the west, and the world rushed in.

By all odds, Sutter should have become one of the world's richest men. He owned an immense area of land adjacent to the richest mining camps. He was a successful farmer with fields of grain and vegetables to sell. He had great herds of sheep and cattle. His fort turned out goods sorely needed by miners.

But it all crumbled. He could hold on to none of it.

His workers took off for the gold fields. His wheat rotted in the fields. Looms lay idle. Leather spoiled in tanning vats. His stock strayed through holes in fences broken by trespassers. Hungry miners slaughtered his cows, trampled his crops. "I had no idea people could be so mean," lamented Sutter.

Sutter himself couldn't adjust to his changed circumstances. He couldn't get past the picture of himself as a land baron. Still playing the gracious host to everyone, he was overwhelmed by the sheer logistics of feeding them.

To compound his troubles, his creditors (and there were many) started demanding immediate payment.

But here Sutter's past bobbed up to save him. His 22-year-old son appeared unexpectedly at the adobe headquarters. To escape his creditors, Sutter put everything in his son's name.

To raise money, John Jr. joined forces with entrepreneur Sam Brannan, had the waterfront land surveyed into lots and sold them for $500 apiece. It was Brannan who named the new townsite Sacramento.

By the end of 1849 Sutter sold out his fort for $40,000. For the rest of his life he continued to lose money through poor judgment and ill luck.

SACRAMENTO: BOOMTOWN ON THE RIVER

By June of that historic year, 1849, the tide of immigration had turned into a flood, and Sacramento was the bustling hub.

Speculation in building lots reached a furious pitch. In June the newspaper reported a hundred houses and 25 stores were "already erected and others going up rapidly." Two weeks later (to show how rapid

that development was) the paper announced, "Sacramento now has 2,000 inhabitants and about 200 houses." The lots that the junior John Sutter had sold with such satisfaction for $500 in January, now commanded $5,000.

Before the year was out, Sacramento had grown to 12,000 people. And even more gold seekers camped outside the town in a sea of tents. They were ragged, gaunt men who had crossed the deserts and mountains, who talked of what they had endured and what they should do next to get to the diggings.

During the winter rainy season, most miners came down from the hills to idle away time in Sacramento. One such was Isaac Lor, who arrived paddling a small boat down the river. "The first that strikes one's attention," he recorded in his diary, "is the want of order, the utter confusion which prevails. The streets are not graded, nor is anything done to clear out the debris. The town is covered with boxes and barrels, wagons, lumber, glass bottles, and plunder. Streets are half a leg deep

in filth and mud, one great cesspool of offal, garbage, and dead animals. I saw one establishment with over 200 boxes of herrings rotting in a pile, and any amount of spoiled pork and moldy cheese.''

It was a great time to be a merchant. Prices were inflated shamelessly by every shopkeeper, and a fortune was virtually promised to anyone with something to sell.

One of the first buildings at the waterfront was erected by slick entrepreneur Sam Brannan, a backsliding Mormon elder who made his stake by collecting tithes from the miners and using the money for his own benefit. Like other merchants whose shops lined the river, he sold picks and shovels and miners' supplies at gouging prices. Mining pans originally priced at 20 cents could now be bought at Brannan's for one ounce of gold dust -- $8 to $16.

Saloons flourished.

According to contemporary historian John Morse, ''The first saloon in town was built from a sail taken from a ship at the Embarcadero. The saloon-keeper wrapped it around three times, put a plank across two barrels, and 'opened' an hour after his arrival. When summer's heat reached the salt-stained canvas walls, miners dubbed his saloon the 'Stinking Tent.'''

Gambling also flourished, here as anywhere else miners gathered. Away from the family fireside, it became an all-absorbing pursuit.

Among the infamous gaming houses, the Round Tent was popular because it displayed erotic pictures on its canvas walls. The Plains was frescoed with paintings of scenes familiar to miners from the overland trail. Prospectors, still dusty from the diggings, brought their heavy sacks of dust and nuggets to the monte tables, where there were tiny scales to weigh out the bets.

But a miner could do more than sin in Sacramento.

He could buy or trade a horse, stock up on canned goods, or take in a play at the Eagle Theater. He could consult one of the numerous "lawyers" (who may or may not have gone to law school), or see a "doctor" (whose medical knowledge may have come from hanging around a drug store).

Gold was the accepted medium of exchange. Wrote miner Isaac Lord, "I was struck aback when I saw the merchants receiving and handling gold. If the dust looks clean, it is poured into the scales and weighed. If it looks dirty and has sand in it, they stir it in their palm with a finger and decide its value. It is poured out and weighed almost as carelessly as pepper in the States, and very few ever pick up any scattering flakes. In larger establishments it is dipped in pint cups. In a word, it is an article of produce, as easily got as wheat, and handled with much the same feeling and same waste."

By the end of 1849 Sacramento was no longer an outpost. Structures lined the waterfront, including hotels, stores, saloons and a theater. The river bank and Embarcadero bustled with people, animals and ships.

Sacramento had moved from the wilderness John Sutter found to a city in a brief 10 years.

COLOMA, WHERE ALL THE FUSS BEGAN

The nugget Marshall picked up the morning of Jan. 24, 1848 was worth no more than fifty cents. But it triggered an inundation of scrambling fortune-seekers that, according to one account, "followed the track of gold like you'll see chickens follow a trail of corn, pecking and scratching away after it." The contagious fever gripped every able-bodied man in the country.

Before the state of madness subsided, almost a billion dollars worth of gold would be wrested from the Sierra foothills.

Newcomers to the diggings learned the business of panning from the "old-timers" (men who may have learned their trade not more than two months previous).

It was a queer scene they walked in on, these newcomers, like nothing they had seen before. The whole of the region was in a ferment. An anthill, just disturbed by some sudden alarm, affords apt illustration of the frenzy that invaded the entire population. Parties of miners flowed by in a continuous current. Everyone was afraid he should be too late, that he should not go to the richest placers, that he should not find the fortune intended for him, that he shouldn't be able to return home the coming winter - in short, that he should not improve the present golden opportunity to the very utmost.

Marshall himself found no more gold. His lament in later years was that it had been "a discovery that hasn't been of much benefit to me." Although he never completely abandoned his pan, prospecting proved to be a futile venture for him.

His momentous discovery altered the course of a nation. But Marshall died penniless and alone, a bitter alcoholic. In the end, he picked up pen money selling his autograph.

The town that grew up near his sawmill became the first white settlement in the foothills. Although the first wave of gold-harvesters didn't hit the dirt until May, Coloma by midsummer boasted a hotel and perhaps as many as 300 frame buildings under construction - most of them made from lumber cut at Sutter's sawmill. Yet, the frenzied diggers threatened to dismantle the very sawmill that was supplying the lumber, in the hope there might be gold underneath it.

It wasn't a ridiculous idea, as far as that goes. That first year, gold seemed to be everywhere. One day the boys were holding a proper funeral for a miner who had died. As they stood around the grave, hats in hand, listening to the solemn eulogy of a preacher-turned-miner, someone spotted "color." One glimpse was enough. The body was moved elsewhere, and everyone grabbed shovel and pick.

There were hundreds of tales to tell around the campfire at night. The joke of it was that most of them were true. None of them, not even the wildest, differed much from that first report made to President Polk by Colonel Mason.

In the summer of '48 there were two thousand men scrambling over the Coloma hillside. In 1849 there were ten thousand.

It was no vacation outing. Digging for gold was backaching, wearisome work. When James Carson first arrived at Mormon Island, a sandbar near the sawmill, he complained, "I worked fifty panfuls of dirt and recovered fifty cents worth of gold." Yet that small spit of land proved so rich that it yielded gold in quantities measured by the pint and half-pint.

It was in Coloma that the tradition of outrageous prices was established. It took a lot of dust to pay for the necessities of life, and merchants like Sam Brannan grew rich.

But miners in town for supplies always had a spree, whatever the cost. Plenty more where that came from! One prospector, paying for his goods, dropped a nugget. A new arrival in town picked it up and offered it to its owner. The man looked at him in astonishment. "Well, stranger," he said, "you are a curiousity! I guess you haven't been here long. Better keep that lump for a sample!"

Coloma in 1848 knew almost no crime. By 1849 the picture had changed. Coloma was described as "a place of marked cards, loaded dice, and false weights."

In 1855 Coloma was the scene of a celebrated double hanging. Hangings were by no means uncommon in 1855, but this affair was done up in grand style, with brass bands and a spirit of revelry. The two principals (one a teacher who had done away with a young lady who rejected him, and the other an ordinary badman) were themselves caught up in the festive spirit. The teacher sang several verses of a song he had composed, and went to the Hereafter with a glorious cry, "Here I come, Susan!". The badman, not to be outdone by an amateur, performed a lively jig - before the noose snuffed out his life.

But it soon became apparent to many that Marshall's site was not the richest on the hill. Coloma's hectic days were numbered. Richer claims elsewhere were soon drawing the restless gold hunters. In late 1851 a visitor called Coloma "the dullest mining town in the whole country."

COLOMA TODAY

The State-operated 220-acre Gold Discovery Site Historic Park now encompasses 70 percent of the town. A highlight is a working reproduction of Sutter's mill, built of rustic lumber, some of it hand-adzed and put together with oak pins by local citizens. The one that John Marshall built has long since faded into oblivion, board by board. A few of the original timbers have been unearthed over the years, now on display at an excellent museum a block from the mill. The museum also offers an entertaining and informative film account of Gold Rush history.

High on a wooded hill above town the trim figure of Marshall on a granite base eternally points a stern bronze finger at the gold discovery site below.

A short walk from the monument, almost hidden in the woods, is the painfully simple, gray clapboard cabin where Marshall lived.

On main street, the store where Frank Bekeart sold guns and ammunition to the '49ers still stands, along with a Chinese store and a Mormon cabin exhibit. Just south of the park, a country inn known as Vineyard House has wine cellars dating from 1860, and a reputation for being haunted by the ghost of Robert Chalmers, second husband of the widow Louisa Althoff.

Sunday morning in the Mines.

Coloma was once the county seat, despite the wails of nearby Hangtown. In those lusty mining days, voting was informal to say the least. There's a story that one eager Coloma booster copied a passenger list from a steamer docked in San Francisco and cast a vote in the name of each for his home town.

No such picturesque activity takes place these days, though. Coloma slumbers in the foothill sun, shaded by locust and mimosa, in the curve of the historic American River. Stilled are the shouts of ten thousand miners who came with their dreams.

HANGTOWN, RICH AND RIBALD

The aim of the prospector was to get as much gold as could be gotten, in the least time possible. It was a restless breed of young men. If they didn't find gold right away, or enough of it, they'd take off for somewhere else and try again. No disease was more widespread than "lump fever," brought on by news, no matter how unreliable, of a big strike some place other than where a miner was working.

So, when Indians brought news of a rich placer on the south fork of the American that was yielding six ounces per day per man, it didn't take long for the men who were digging holes around Coloma to pack up blanket and bottle and set off across the hills.

That was June, 1848. Instantly, the success stories started piling one on another. Will Daylor and Perry McCoon, it was said, panned $17,000 in one week, and some claims were yielding five pounds a day.

But in July an awkward situation developed in the diggings. Stream levels fell so low there wasn't enough water to wash the dirt, and men were obliged to pack sacks of dirt on their backs and lug them down to the creek for panning. That earned the town its first name: Dry Diggins (later changed to Old Dry Diggins).

Rich diggings had a way of attracting unsavory characters, and Dry Diggins had its share. That first winter, three transients were tried for robbery and attempted murder (there are several versions of the crimes but only one of the punishment), and were summarily hanged. That earned the town its new name: Hangtown.

The first recorded Gold Country lynching took place at Old Dry Diggins. Three "foreigners" had been caught trying to rob a gambler, Edward Buffum, and were given 39 lashes each for that crime. Then someone said he was sure those were the same men who had murdered a miner at Stanislaus the previous summer. Weak from the lashings, and unable to understand English, the prisoners offered no defense. Within the half-hour they had been tried, sentenced, and hanged.

Buffum tried to stop it. "I mounted a stump and in the name of God, humanity, and the law protested against such a course of proceeding, but the crowd, by this time excited by frequent and deep potations of liquor from a neighboring groggery, would listen to nothing contrary to their brutal desires, and even threatened to hang me if I did not immediately desist from any further remarks."

Fortunately, the name Hangtown didn't stick. Eventually, decorum prevailed and the name was changed to Placerville.

In the autumn of 1848, Edward Buffum took his first try at prospecting near Hangtown. "I shall never forget," he wrote in his diary, "the delight with which I struck and worked out a crevice. It appeared to be filled with a hard gravel, which I took out with my knife, and there at the bottom, strewn along the whole length of the rock, was bright yellow gold, in little pieces about the size of a grain of barley. Oh, how my heart beat! I sat still and looked at it some minutes before I touched it."

Dry Diggins, that first summer, was "the happiest set of men on earth," according to one miner's account. By autumn it was a thriving camp with wooden stores, surging traffic, and a main street a mile long. A visitor to the town, J.D. Borthwick, was astonished to discover that this main street was not only a thoroughfare, but also a mining camp. Someone had struck pay dirt there, and parties of energetic miners had converged with pick and shovel.

"Here and there, in the middle of the street," he reported, "would be a square hole about six feet deep, in which one miner was digging while another was bailing the water out with a bucket, and a third, sitting alongside the heap of dirt which had been dug up, was washing it with a rocker."

Borthwick made note also, that the street was "plentifully strewed with old boots, hats, old sardine boxes, empty oyster tins, empty bottles, worn-out pots and kettles, old ham bones, and other rubbish too various to particularize."

Families arrived to augment the strictly male population of 1848. A doctor arrived in '49 with his wife - a delicate French lady born in Paris, it was said. But crossing the prairies, the doctor had an accident that laid him up, and it was the "delicate French lady" who walked beside the wagon for the last 800 miles, managing the team of oxen. "She arrived in the best of health and spirits," it was reported.

Of somewhat hardier persuasion was Miss "Immigrant Jane" Stuart, who made her stake driving a herd of horses across the plains, and used that stake to buy a house on Main Street and set up a bawdy house operation.

A miner in Hangtown, upgrading himself from beans, asked the cook to fry up a mixture of three of the countryside's most expensive products - eggs, bacon and oysters. Thus was created a concoction known as Hangtown Fry, destined to be seen on menus in the classiest restaurants in the country.

Placerville attracted a colorful assortment of early citizens, some of whom became rich and famous. Mark Hopkins opened a grocery store with a single wagonload of supplies, and launched a career that tied him in with Collis Huntington selling shovels (for which the Forty-Niners paid dearly), and later gave him an opportunity to run a little railroad known as the Central Pacific.

Twenty-year-old Philip Armour left his family farm in New York in 1849 and walked to California, a project that took six months. It took another five years to get together $8,000, enough to open a modest butcher shop. Supplying meat for hungry miners proved profitable, and Armour discovered his own golden stake right next to the diggings.

Another fortune that blossomed out of the gold dust was made by John Studebaker. He left his business of making Conestoga wagons in Indiana, crossing the plains in one of his own products (which he later sold for $300). He took a job forging wheelbarrows and worked for five years to save enough money to go back to South Bend and become an automobile tycoon.

And it was from Hangtown, in 1853, that the famous skiing mailman, Snowshoe Thompson, started his 20-year run (largely unpaid) delivering mail and supplies between Nevada and California. His service became a vital link when silver was struck in Virginia City in 1859.

And it was that same discovery that made Placerville a transportation center in reverse; the tide of humanity that once streamed westward for gold now turned around and streamed eastward for silver, making Placerville the outfitting point for the rush to Washoe.

As Nevada boomed, so did Placerville. Streets were thronged with noisy crowds, waiting impatiently for stage coaches and mule trains that were booked up days in advance. Hotels overflowed, saloons were stampeded. The hills surrounding the city were piled with boxes waiting to be sent over the Sierra. Five thousand teams clogged the road to Virginia City, bringing back silver bullion on the return trip.

When the Comstock bubble burst, so did Placerville's prosperity. The town survived as a pleasant trading center nestled in a ravine, its winding streets still following the original mule paths.

PLACERVILLE TODAY

A disastrous fire (so common to the early camps) leveled most of Placerville's original buildings. But some escaped. One of the holdovers, built in the early 1850's, is at 524 Main Street. The Placerville Hardware building at 441 Main dates back to 1856. And the handsome building erected by Immigrant Jane with her earnings from herding horses, still stands at 489 Main. The City Hall occupies a building that was once the focus of the town's social life, home of the famous firefighting company. Confidence Engine Company Number One.

Some of the town's early citizens are buried in a cemetery at the edge of town; but they will be forever anonymous, since fire, the common enemy, didn't respect the dead any more than it did the living.

Placerville may be the only town in the West to have taken on a mine as a civic attraction. The Gold Bug Mine, a mile up Bedford Avenue, is open to the public, fully lighted for easy exploring. The lower shaft is 360 feet long, glittering with gold bearing quartz.

Placerville today is more given to agriculture than mining. And its hills are covered with apple trees instead of mine shafts. In the autumn, when the trees are heavy with fruit, the orchards become a carnival site, as thousands of visitors meander through Apple Hill to buy crunchy apples off the trees, or to sample the best apple pastry of the farmer's wife.

AUBURN, RAVINE OF RICHES

Once gold mania had set in at Coloma, avid gold seekers fanned out and swarmed over the surrounding countryside. With amazing energy they pushed their way up the rivers and creeks, dug into every nook and cranny. The region flanking the original discovery site got first attention.

An Australian named Yankee Jim worked his way upriver from Coloma; one of the richest diggings became a town named after him.

And a friend of James Marshall, Claude Chana, unexpectedly found himself the founder of a mining camp that grew into the city of Auburn. Chana was on his way to the Coloma diggings with three Frenchmen and a party of Indians when he decided to stop in the ravine and practice with his mining pan. He came up with three good-sized nuggets on his first attempt.

In less than a week, Auburn had sprouted.

Like most mining camps, it went by several names before settling into something permanent. For a while it was Wood's Dry Diggins, then North Fork Dry Diggins, then Rich Dry Diggins. In '49 some roving New Yorkers, feeling nostalgic, named it after their home town, Auburn. That stuck.

The original settlement began at the bottom of the ravine. But by 1850 some 1500 men had gradually straggled up the hillside, in their everlasting search for a better spot, and a second town developed at a higher level. This is the Auburn that remains today.

The town in the ravine came to a spectacular end one summer's day in 1855 when a ravaging fire took just one hour and twenty-five minutes to remove Old Auburn from the face of Placer County.

Auburn's surface placers were quickly exhausted, and it took an accidental discovery to keep the town booming. A miner named Jenkins had built a ditch to carry water to his diggings in Missouri Gulch. When the water mysteriously stopped flowing, he investigated and found it was pouring into a gopher hole above his claim. Looking closely, he saw that the bottom was covered with coarse gold. In a month, Jenkins took $40,000 out of that gopher hole.

Hiram Pierce made the agonizing crossing through the Isthmus, and started his digging along the American River near Auburn:

"Arrived at the diggins. The Senery is wild in the extreme. Smith and myself made a tent. The gold at this place seems diffused through all the Earth but is verry fine.
"Rose and got breckfast. At 11 attended preaching under a live oak by a Congregational Minister from New Bedford. Went to work. Made a small show. All of us got much less than an ounce. It is verry much like work. Potatoes $1 a piece, onions the same. At night the Wolves and Kiotas give us plenty of music.

"Went out prospecting & find that every foot of Ground has been turned over. It is a most wild and romantic Sene. We bake pancakes, fry pork, drink Coffey & sleep on the Ground. It is verry warm during the day. The wolves stole some meat from a neighbor's tent, taking it from within a foot or two of his head. We got 2 small loaves of bread baked at a Mormon family that arrived overland. They charged $1 per loaf for baking & verry heavy hard bread at that. Wrote home & sent a rough drawing of the digins and one dollars worth of gold dust. My back getting lame in consequence, as I think, of getting my feet wet & sleeping on ground. Daniel Newcom has a verry sore hand caused by poison, Smith has a sort of felon on his hand caused by rubbing on the cradle, & Haskins hands & feet are sore from Scurvey & sunburnt."

The election process seemed to be a never-failing diversion for the entertainment-starved men of early mining camps. When an election was held in 1850 to determine the county seat, Auburn citizens, feeling frisky about their thriving, go-ahead town, set up polls in the general store, and with the promise of "free refreshments" lured voters from far and near to come and do their civic duty (cast a ballot for Auburn). The election was so successful that Auburn's majority was larger than the county's whole population!

Life was lively in those rambunctious times, everybody trying to turn up gold one way or another. Some, like "Rattlesnake Dick," found that the most convenient way to pick up spare cash was by robbing stagecoaches. This outlaw, who got his name from the fact that he had once been a miner on Rattlesnake Bar, plundered stages with considerable success for six years. Although he was occasionally captured and put away, he never did find jails to his liking and somehow always managed to slip out.

After authorities had put up with that for six years, they got understandably sore about his shenanigans. On one occasion, a deputy from Auburn got word that Rattlesnake Dick and a companion had bought tickets and boarded a stage in Nevada City, as cool as though they were honest men, and were headed for Auburn. The deputy, thinking to make a hero of himself, waylaid the stage and came forward to arrest the bandits. But the badmen were unimpressed with his demonstration of authority, and with great aplomb demanded to see the warrant. While the diligent officer searched his pockets, Dick calmly shot him. That chore out of the way, the outlaws made a few nasty remarks about unfriendly Placer County, and left the stage.

But Rattlesnake Dick, cool as he was, met his comeuppance. One night, while riding boldly down Auburn's main street, he was challenged by a posse and shot to death.

The rich gold deposits played out in Auburn, as they did everywhere, but the town survived because it was a key center along the routes to the mines and across the Sierra. Dozens of trails radiated from the heart of town to the mining camps.

Its position as a transportation hub became even more firmly entrenched when Central Pacific's first passenger arrived in town in 1865.

The hills and valleys around Auburn are a monument to the humor of the Forty-Niner in attaching ludicrous names to the diggings. Most are gone without a trace, but there was once a Shirt Tail Canyon, a Drunkard's Bar, a Ladies' Canyon, and a Dell's Delight.

AUBURN TODAY

Some of the finest remnants of the most glorious adventure in California's history are to be found in Auburn's Old Town. Even the willy-nilly pattern of the streets is a memory of the past, when streets were simply paths to somebody's diggins. They angle off in every direction, with hardly a square block in town.

Commercial Street has been Lawyer's Row since the turbulent early days of Auburn. The nearby Masonic Hall was once George Willment's general store, with the Masons using the upper story. The old Placer County Bank building was built after the fire of 1855. And the Union Bar at the end of the street was in the 1850's one of the wildest saloons in wild Auburn.

The white dome of the Court House dominates the horizon from anywhere in town, but it dates back only to 1893, when it replaced the former site of justice, the public hanging grounds. Inside, a 60-foot spiral staircase leads to two circular rooms in the dome.

The most interesting relic in town is the old Firehouse, a four-story, red-and-white wonder with a steeply pitched tower that culminates in a cupola. Like the Court House, it dates back to 1893. But the Auburn Hook & Ladder Company that occupied it was organized back in 1852.

Auburn Firehouse

There was once a sizable community of Chinese in Auburn, and the remnants of their existence can be found on the steep slope of Sacramento Street.

Every June, Auburn strikes a path back to the 19th century and celebrates Chana's discovery of gold nuggets in his pan, and the gold rush madness that followed. And while they're at it, they celebrate the demise of Rattlesnake Dick.

OTHER DIGGINGS

Most California mining towns followed a similar pattern: rapid growth, rapid decline. A town was born when some prospector squatting on some lonely hillside locus, discovered pay dirt in his pan. Within weeks the spot became a full-fledged town with saloon and general store. The town was named after anything handy to the miner's humor - Ben Hur, Sweet Revenge, Chicken Thief Flat. Some names were unprintable.

If the gold petered out, or if sufficient color showed up elsewhere, the entire canvas city simply moved, and any wooden structures were generally obliterated from the scenery by the inevitable fire. If a church was built, generally its spire was all that remained.

GEORGETOWN...Gold was discovered here by an Englishman, George Phipps. At the shout of "Gold!" a tent city quickly popped up, christened Growlersburg by the miners because the gravels were so rich the pans "growled with nuggets."

Several historic buildings remain: Wells Fargo; the Balser House, built in 1859 when Charles Balser married the "widder Olmstead," the Shannon Knox House, oldest in town, built from lumber that came around the Horn. The town has many other charming homes and old-fashioned gardens dating from the Victorian era, and a picturesque old hotel.

FOLSOM...By spring of 1848 there wasn't a riverside spot within twenty miles of Coloma that hadn't been poked, picked and pried by men who had formerly classed themselves as lumber mill hands.

Wherever they found signs of gold, settlements developed. Along the south fork of the American there was Morman Island, Big and Little Negro Hills, and Salmon Falls. At Negro Bar, where luck was running good, a cluster of tents and shacks appeared, loosely resembling a town.

But like so many transitory camps, Negro Bar was destined for a short life. Another town was developing on the bluff above, a town that would be called Granite City, and later Folsom. Negro Bar was inundated, and today lies beneath Nimbus Lake.

PILOT HILL...This is the landmark that guided John Fremont back from the Sierra mountains.

The most remarkable sight is the graceful three-story hotel built by Alonzo Bayley when he heard the railroad was coming through. It didn't. And Bayley turned to agriculture and organized California's first grange. "Bayley's Folly" looks like a misplaced Louisiana mansion, and is considered one of the most fascinating buildings in the Mother Lode country.

VOLCANO ERUPTION
It is remarkable how swiftly the rush for riches spread across the gold-laden hills. Although the first wave of argonauts didn't start digging at Coloma until May in 1848, by autumn the tidal wave had inundated the entire foothill strip until it was alive with the shouts and curses of 10,000 miners. Men whose only previous contact with gold had been no more than owning a gold pocket watch, suddenly were in the business of mining it. That brief summer of '48 saw new beginnings in hundreds of locations, all started by men who knew nothing about what they were doing but who shook pans of muck and rock until they (sometimes) became rich.

It was about midsummer when Col. Jonathon Stevenson and some troops of the New York Volunteers (remnants of the war just ended) wandered into a craggy gulch some distance from the Marshall discovery site, and found placers and clay beds so rich that the soldiers were averaging $100 a day. The camp was dubbed Soldiers Gulch.

The following year gold seekers poured into the new camp from every direction, and because the crags resembled volcanic rock, the name was changed to Volcano.

A town of 5,000 sprang up; they cleaned out $90 million in gold from the rocks by sluicing (and later hydraulicking) before everyone gave up and walked away from the town's 17 hotels, 35 saloons, three breweries, and two temperance societies.

"Salting" claims with a few well-placed nuggets was not uncommon for men who liked to make a little profit selling their claims. None was more adept at it than Moore Lerty. He stuffed his musket with a few nuggets, shot them into the earth, and then sold the worthless real estate for a thousand dollars to some unsuspecting newcomer. His con artistry backfired on him, though, when he sold to Henry Jones. The Jones claim proved to be the best in camp, yielding not only the $200 worth of nuggets that Lerty had donated, but a few thousand more.

During the Civil War, Volcano was a hotbed of spirit. At one point, Union loyalists in town discovered that some Confederate sympathizers were planning to rob Wells Fargo and use the money for the Confederate cause. The Union Blues rolled out an old cannon that had been left behind from the Mexican War (just ended) and hauled it down the street to save the town for the Union. They had no cannon balls, and no one knew how to discharge it. But one Mexican War veteran said he'd seen it done. They stuffed the cannon with rocks and held the Confederates at bay without a shot.

Later they learned they'd have blown up the whole town if they'd lit the fuse.

Frontier justice was always known for being quick and to the point. The opening of a new saloon in Volcano was obvious cause for a gala celebration. But when the men decided the owner was overcharging for his whiskey, they cut a hole in the roof, hoisted the proprietor up, and let him dangle there while they enjoyed a few drinks on the house. He was soon convinced that his prices might be too high.

VOLCANO TODAY

Many of Volcano's original buildings still line the street in a state of arrested decay. All the buildings are genuine; there are no replicas or restorations.

The handsome, three-storied St. George Hotel which looms prominently at the entrance to town, has remained active and well patronized over the years. Down the street there are a number of ancient stone buildings housing various enterprises such as a rock shop, a book store, and an ice cream parlor called the Jug and Rose.

California's first public library was established in Volcano, but it failed, as a newspaper report said, "because the Association had no power to compel the restitution of books."

At the end of the block, the patriotic cannon, Old Abe, is housed in an old shed next door to the Union Hotel (once the Union Billiard Saloon and Boarding House).

One of the stone breweries survives from 1856, and there are partial buildings, well marked, that once represented Wells Fargo, a door factory and the business address of a lost generation of women who struck their own unique claims. The jail remains. Its first customers were the two men who built it.

A couple of miles out of town, up Ram's Horn Grade, there's a hill that turns gold with daffodils every spring. Early Dutch settlers, bringing a touch of home with them, planted the first bulbs. Now the yellow flowers cover four acres every spring.

The County Jail at Jackson attained a fame of sorts for its worthlessness. An editorial of the day claimed it was "made of logs so small that a man could cut his way out in an hour or two with his jack knife, and moreover, the logs are so rotten that an enterprising pig could root his way out."

36

MURPHYS, A SOLDIER'S FORTUNE

When the Seventh Regiment of New York Volunteers found they had arrived too late for the war, they decided to try a little mining. They worked Weber Creek (near Placerville) for a while. But when the claims started yielding less than three ounces a day, George Angel and the two Murphy brothers, who were in the party, decided to strike out. Jim Carson joined them. Heading south, they mined streams along the way, finding gold in almost all of them.

When they reached the stream now known as Angels Creek, George Angel decided to settle there. The group broke up...Carson headed south. And the Murphy boys turned easterly, found a likely spot on a creek being worked by a few Indians, and set up a trading tent.

John Murphy was only 23 years old, but he had one very useful talent. He was able to convince the Indians to do his digging for him. In return for their work, he supplied them with goods from his trading post. For example, when one of the Indians gave him a five-pound lump of gold, he gave him a blanket in return.

Perhaps his success at public relations with the Indians could be partially explained by a report of a man who visited the diggings in October, 1848: "They respect his person and property in part due to the fact he married the daughter of the chief."

At any rate, things appeared to go well for the Murphys, since early records show the brothers took $1.5 million worth of gold that autumn of '48.

And inasmuch as the rich diggings had brought such a rush of prospectors that claims were limited to eight square feet, it is safe to assume the Murphys were also doing a lively business in the trading tent.

To become millionaires and instant capitalists before age 25 gave the Murphy boys a head start on life. They both went on to greater victories; John went from mining into politics, and Daniel parlayed his dust into holdings of some three million acres in cattle land.

Meanwhile, fifteen miles to the north of Murphys, a grove of mammoth Sequoia pine trees was discovered by A.T. Dowd, who was called a liar for his pains. Later, a remarkably enterprising promoter named Gale took it upon himself to prove the truth of Dowd's claims. He peeled a 116-foot strip of bark from one of the trees and toured it around the country on exhibit.

Suddenly, everyone wanted to go and visit the Big Trees. And so, at a time when mining at Murphys Flat was beginning to wane, the town found itself the gateway to a popular tourist attraction.

This is undoubtedly what prompted James Sperry (of the flour family) to build, in 1854, a luxury hotel on Main Street. For its time, it was a marvel of elegance in the diggings.

Everyone, it seemed, wanted to stay at the Sperry & Perry Hotel. General Grant slept there (but then he appears to have slept in every city in the West where there was gold, silver, or a saloon). Author Horatio Alger signed the register, as did Count A. von Rothschild.

But the guest whose stay lived on in memory was C.E. Bolton, a quiet, scholarly person whose later fame derived from the fact he earned his livelihood as a highwayman called Black Bart.

Unfortunately, the Sperry & Perry Hotel, touted as being impervious to fire, went down with the rest in the holocaust of 1859, despite thick stone walls and iron shutters. It was hastily rebuilt, more elegant than ever, and has passed through a few ownerships since the Messrs. Sperry and Perry left the scene.

MURPHYS TODAY

The Sperry & Perry is still that same gracious balconied hostelry with massive iron shutters, but it is now known as Murphys Hotel.

Across the street, in the Travers building (oldest structure in town, dating back to 1856) there's a superb, backwoodsy Old-Timer Museum, put together by the eminent historian Dr. R. Coke Wood. There are plenty of other buildings of interest in the locust-shaded town - the Jones Apothecary Shop, the ever-present Wells Fargo building, and a one-room jail.

One of the most charming structures is the Murphys Elementary School which was, until it closed in 1973, the oldest continuously used grammar school in California. It's now an official historic monument, but in more urgent times it provided the basic Three-Rs to a future Nobel Prize winner, Albert Michelson, who in 1907 became the first American to achieve that honor in physics.

Four miles out of Murphys, on the Vallecito-Columbia highway, there's a fantastic formation called Moaning Cavern, which miners stumbled onto in 1851. Never willing to pass up a chance to prospect new diggings, the miners daringly lowered themselves into the vast cavern by long ropes, hoping to find the elusive rich vein of gold. Instead of gold, they found a remarkable chamber of natural limestone, big enough to hold a twelve-story building. It was filled with gigantic, crystalline formations.

Today it has been made easily accessible to tourists, who descend an all-steel spiral staircase a hundred feet to the floor of the main chamber, where they are surrounded by 300 million years of spectacular geological history.

Another underground cavern, even more wildly magnificent, was discovered about the same time by miners on the old wagon trail from Murphys to Mokelumne Hill. One day the prospectors were target practicing, and when the target needed moving they discovered the opening to the cave. It quickly became the must-see tourist attraction of the times. A hotel was built, and a lively gold town called Cave City developed.

But Cave City died. Its handsome hotel sagged into the earth. The forest and brush choked out civilization, and the entrance to the cave was sealed. Only recently it has been rediscovered and more fully explored. New rooms eighty feet high were discovered, along with subterranean lakes 250 feet deep. Once again, tourists are exploring its strange beauty, this time on limited tours conducted by Sierra Nevada Recreation Corp., (Vallecito), and discovering, like John Muir, "charming lakes of unknown depths, downgrowing crystals arranged in graceful flowing folds plicated like silken drapery."

ANGELS CAMP, HEART OF THE LODE

While John and Daniel Murphy were making the Golden Dream come true in the town that bears their name, another bearded ex-soldier in the ragged uniform of Stevenson's volunteers - George Angel - was prospering at Angels Camp. He had stopped to mine a creek whose golden riches were in plain sight, available to any man with sufficient energy to pick up the flakes. That was the sort of gold these first arrivals, utterly ignorant of the rudiments of mining, were seeking.

But like the Murphys, George Angel found his gold in selling overpriced items to other men who were mucking for gold. As the miners prospered, so did the trading post.

That first summer, the population of Angels Camp was reported as "300 exclusive of Indians." A year later that figure jumped to 4,500. The hills were dotted with tents, and the creeks filled with human beings to such a degree that it seemed as if a day's work of the mass would not leave a stone unturned in them.

This is the area where the term "Mother Lode" first came into usage in 1851. It refers to the Veta Madre which the Mexicans claimed existed, from which a series of veins supposedly sprouted and extended along the western slope of the Sierra from Coulterville to Georgetown, passing right through Angels Camp.

One of the most spectacular discoveries in Angels Camp, the kind legends are made of, was the unexpected wealth of one of the town's characters, Bennager Raspberry, a storekeeper on Main Street. Originally Raspberry's fame sprang from the fact that he had ordered a case of brandied peaches (miners who struck it rich appreciated the little niceties of life) that had spoiled on the long trip around the Horn. He dumped the spoiled peaches out behind his store, and all the pigs in Angels Camp were roaring drunk for four days and nights.

But Raspberry hit it rich in something besides peaches. One day he was having trouble with a jammed rifle. Attempting to correct the problem, he shot the gun into the ground. The ramrod dashed against a rock and broke it open, revealing a sizable gold deposit. Within three days Raspberry had scraped $10,000 worth of gold dust out of the rocky ground.

Mark Twain spent time in Angels Camp in the 1860s. It was in the Angels Hotel that he heard a tale from Ross Coon, the bartender, about a frog contest that became the basis for "The Celebrated Jumping Frog of Calaveras," a story that launched both Twain and Angels Camp into fame.

According to the yarn, an inveterate gambler named Smiley trained a common garden-variety frog to make phenomenal leaps on command. That night at the saloon he challenged a stranger to produce any frog that could beat Dan'l Webster. The stranger clandestinely fed Dan'l a handful of shot; after that, nothing Smiley did could move Dan'l off his tail.

While Mark Twain was in mining country, he made a multitude of sporadic notes that give a brief glimpse of his stay in Angels Camp. In particular, he was critical of the food at Hotel Angels, and described the coffee as "day-before-yesterday dishwater." On January 23, 1865, he noted, "Beans and dishwater for breakfast at the Frenchman's. Dishwater and beans for dinner. And both articles warmed over for supper." On February 3 his notes indicate that hellfire soup had been added to the menu, one of four recipes the cook had for making soup. Others: general debility, insanity, and sudden death.

The story probably would have been forgotten with the passing of time. But in 1928 Angels Camp streets were finally paved, and residents decided to celebrate the event with a Jumping Frog Jubilee. The affair became an annual event, and has brought back the whoop-de-doo excitement of Gold Rush times for one spirited week in May.

Bret Harte spent two months in 1855 wandering around the mining camps from Angels Camp southward, and collected enough stories to make him famous. His "Luck of Roaring Camp" was a popular tale of life in a mining camp. But some critics felt he came too late to the party, that the life he depicted was not typical of the early madness. Nevertheless, his stories attained instant popularity, and as editor of Overland Monthly he poured out one after another..."The Outcasts of Poker Flat," "Idyll of Red Gulch," "Bell Ringer of Angels."

Harte admitted that he disliked the rough life of mining camps and found the foothills "ugly, vulgar and lawless."

By the end of the 1850s, many mining camps across the foothills had faded into oblivion. Pickings were lean. There was word of gold in Fraser River. Silver in Nevada. And the restless miners moved on, as miners are inclined to do.

But in Angels Camp, where quartz mining had replaced the earlier sluicing, prosperity continued. Utica Mining Company, organized in the 1850s, was a major source of gold for the next forty years.

Yet, mining in quartz lacks romance; it's an industrial process. And in later years, when miners reminisced about their experiences, they remembered best their achievements with pan, cradle, and tom, in spite of the tedium and discomfort.

They remembered placer mining as a great adventure.

ESPECIALLY DEDICATED TO OUR LADY READERS IN THE EAST.

NEEDS NO COMMENT.

ANGELS CAMP TODAY

Among the most notable remnants of early days are the Angels Hotel and the jailhouse behind it. The Angels mine, one of the best in the area, was located across from the Catholic Church, where only the foundations now remain.

The museum near the north end of town has good collections of minerals and early day artifacts. In the yard outside are an old steam engine, a cannon, and a section of one of the world's largest drill cores.

The city has placed a statue of Mark Twain in a delightful park just outside of town, a great place to picnic and imagine what it was like when hundreds of men in red flannel shirts and battered hats moved a ton of gravel a day to make their beans.

Miners in luck liked to treat themselves to a little luxury to celebrate a strike. One miner, known only as Buckshot, was rumored to have spent an entire $30,000 strike on French champagne and fancy victuals.

Angels Camp, with its high curbed sidewalks, depicts the gracious Victorian atmosphere that followed the rough-and-tumble Gold Rush years. There are three churches that date back to earliest times, and the IOOF building that seems to be part of every Gold Rush town. The swinging doors that once opened to miners at the old Star Saloon, have been transplanted to a restaurant in Altaville, just north of Angels.

SAN ANDREAS COMMOTION

Meanwhile, Mexicans had set up camp a few miles to the north and were panning out dust in considerable quantity. Their good fortune wasn't to last long. When American prospectors discovered how well they were doing, they moved in on the rich diggings, took over the streams, and ran off the "Foreigners."

San Andreas was one of the first settlements to feel the racial clashes that later rocked the mines. (Later, however, when the Yankees no longer found the diggings profitable, they let the patient Chinese come in to scratch for leftovers.)

One of the Mexicans who fell victim to discrimination was Joaquin Murietta, who lived on the outskirts of the diggings. He was horse-whipped, and his brother shot without cause. He took to the outlaw trail, swearing revenge. He robbed where he chose, laughed at the law, and used his income from banditry to aid the poor, in true Robin Hood tradition. Before his career ended, it is said, he killed every man who had mistreated him.

This legend has been challenged by historians, who contend that there was no way one bandit could be in so many places at one time, and that every bad man named either Joaquin or Murietta got credit for being Joaquin Murietta.

Nevertheless, Murietta's career came to a bloody close when he and his partner, Three-Fingered Jack, were killed in a gun battle. Their erstwhile monte partner set up a profitable enterprise by cutting off Joaquin's head and Jack's distinctive hand, pickling them in alcohol, and exhibiting them around the state.

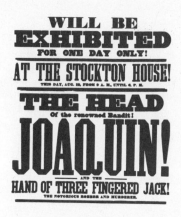

The legend of Joaquin Murietta lived long with old-timers who remembered for years his flamboyance in ordering a bullet-proof vest to be made, which he tested by shooting himself at point-blank range.

Other racial battles erupted. In a nearby area known as Chile Gulch, a number of Chilean miners were working claims. When American miners discovered that a Chilean named Doctor Concha had taken up claims in the names of a number of peons, who were working the claims for his profit, they made it clear to Doctor Concha they had already adopted a ruling that no claims could be held by slaves. Concha responded to that by sending his peons out to attack the Americans in a neighboring gulch. The mines promptly adopted a resolution expelling all Chileans from the diggings. Doctor Concha thereupon got a warrant from the Stockton alcalde for the arrest of the offending Americans. The fight mushroomed into out-and-out battle, with several casualties. The Americans won the Chilean War and confiscated the claims. But the confrontation came close to international complications when both Santiago and Washington got involved in the dispute.

San Andreas started to take on a look of permanence in 1851 when a Frenchman named Banque built the "first brick store" in town. It was, more accurately, a stone-and-adobe building with a facing of brick imported from Stockton. In 1870, Joseph Agostini, a '49er, bought the building, merchandise and all, and added some rooms from brick he made himself, and turned the place into a cheery rooming house for wayfarers who cured homesickness sitting around the fireside eating Mrs. Agonstini's good home cooking.

By 1866 San Andreas had reached a civilized state and made a move to wrest the Calaveras county seat away from Mokelumne Hill - an act accompanied by no small amount of grumbling in Mok Hill when it was discovered that more votes had been cast than there were residents.

After San Andreas had built a courthouse and was in business as a county seat, they had the honor of trying and convicting Black Bart, the foppish stagecoach bandit. Black Bart was a fairly lovable highwayman (to everyone but Wells Fargo) who successfully held up 26 stages before he was caught, betrayed by a laundry mark that led to the revelation he was actually Charles Bolton, a mild-mannered San Francisco clerk. Black Bart never fired a shot during his career as a robber, but of course it was wrong of him to take all that money. And for his crimes he spent six years in the hoosegow.

It took some ingenious contraptions to bring water to the sluice box.

The theatrical bandit, Black Bart, became a celebrity in his own time, providing thousands of column-inches of copy for local newspapers. When he took to leaving bits of poetry at the scene of the crime, his legend was assured.

One of his most famous verses was this literary effort:
I've labored long and hard for bread,
for honor and for riches.
But on my corns too long you've trod,
you fine-haired sons of Bitches.

SAN ANDREAS TODAY

Not much of Gold Rush San Andreas remains, but its Main Street is a narrow, high-sidewalked Mexican style thoroughfare with much charm. The old Courthouse has been restored to its original condition, and contains a fine museum. The jail out back once housed everyone from desperadoes to over-indulging miners. And through its iron doors once passed Black Bart to get his dues.

On the outskirts of town there's a cemetery that saw its first burials as early as 1851. Most of the graves are now unmarked, or the statistics have been worn away by weather and passing years. But some markers tell of the sad end of young men who left their homes to die in a strange land. One grave, apparently containing two bodies, records an unusual end: "Sacred to the memory of James Lagton and Michael Coogan, both natives of Ireland, who came to a premature end by falling of a bank of earth upon them August MDCCLII."

Another bears an inscription that gives insight into the youth of the men who crossed a continent to find the Golden Land: "Here rests the remains of William A. Sampson, aged 22 years, and Robert Bradshaw, aged 21 years, both of Charlestown, Massachusetts. They were cruelly murdered at Chile Gulch, July 18, 1851, by three Mexican assassins for the sake of gold.

The miner's cabin pictured in the Paris Journal Universel (lower picture) is quite different from the reality in the photo above.

WILD MOKELUMNE HILL

Mokelumne Hill, once the county seat of Calaveras County until the honor was appropriated by San Andreas, was inundated by eager miners as early as August, 1848, and because of the richness of its diggings quickly developed into the liveliest, lustiest, nastiest of the mining camps. It was a matter of some bragging that during one 17-week period a man had been killed every weekend, and five had been killed in just one week.

Besides the nearby Chilean War which took their attention briefly, the Mok Hill people enjoyed the excitement of a French War which erupted when a group of Frenchmen found a sizable deposit of gold on a hillside and raised the French flag to celebrate. That made the Americans mad, and without any further reference to mining law, they simply took over the hill, routed the French, and raised "Old Glory." They also appropriated the gold, of course.

There was so much gold available in the surrounding country that indeed it was difficult not to get rich that first summer. One day a Negro miner arrived on the scene and politely inquired where was a good place to dig. The boys, ever ready for a little practical joke, pointed to a hill that had been combed over and picked dry. The newcomer, not realizing he was mining barren soil, hit pay dirt and was seen the following week in town with a poke full of dust.

The gathering of gold and the spending of it took most of the miners' time and energy. But they were not without some interest in the affairs of the country. Bayard Taylor, a New York Tribune correspondent who wandered the mining camps during 1849, chanced to be in Mokelumne

for the first state election in November. "Election day dawned wet and cheerless," he wrote. "Until noon the miners lay dozing idly in their tents, unable to work." At last the voting began in the largest of the tents, which happened to be a saloon...the inspectors being seated behind the counter in close proximity to the glasses and bottles, the calls for which were as frequent as the votes." None of the miners knew who was running for office, yet there was a strong spirit of patriotism, and everyone chose to do his duty by voting. As one miner told Taylor, "When I left home, I was determined to go it blind. I went it blind in coming to California, and I'm not going to stop now. I voted for the Constitution and I've never seen the Constitution. I voted for all the candidates and I don't know a damned one of them. I'm going it blind all through, I am."

Such was the birthday of the new State.

With such a prodigious supply of criminals, Vigilance Committees became the standard form of justice in Mokelumne Hill, as they were elsewhere in 1852. In the minds of those who defended them, they were justified as the only form of crime deterrent that worked.

The San Francisco Herald correspondent in Calaveras County reported on the state of affairs to his editor..."Scarcely a night has passed for some time but some man has been robbed. Last night Perkins was robbed, and a Mexican named Carlos was found on the tent floor, too drunk to explain his errand. He staggered off, but was soon discovered sober, and was arrested by the committee. He had enough gold in his possession that Perkins could identify as his lately stolen gold." What to do with Carlos? They could commit him to the Jackson jail, but "if he remained 24 hours it would only be because he liked the accommodations and had no fear of being convicted. If we hung him, there would be one thief less." The committee elected to hang him, and Carlos made no objection, but asked only for "a good supper, a priest, and a glass of brandy." He slept well and walked coolly to his gallows next morning, even cheerfully helping about his own execution.

Most of the miners were young men. They seldom were called by their real names, but were nicknamed Sailor Jack, Fuzzy, Red Rover, Dutch Jake, Pious Pete. It was not always healthy or polite to inquire too closely into a man's background unless he volunteered it. A popular ditty in the gold fields was:
Oh, what was your name in the States?
Was it Thompson, or Johnson or Bates?
Did you flee for your life,
Or murder your wife?
Say, what was your name in the States?

In 1854 Mokelumne Hill claimed a population of 15,000. Miners were raking it in so fast that they could afford luxuries not common to the average prospector in the foothills. "It was no unusual thing," reported Bayard Taylor, "to see a company of these men who had never before had a thought of luxury beyond a good beefsteak and a glass of whiskey, drinking their champagne at ten dollars a bottle, and eating their canned tongue and sardines, or warming up in the smoky camp kettle their tin cannisters of turtle soup and lobster salad."

Prosperity in the diggings was always accompanied by escalating prices in stores and restaurants. At one hotel a slice of bread cost a dollar (buttered, two dollars).

Keeping a mule wasn't exactly cheap, either. Barley went for a dollar a quart, grass a dollar a handful.

At one time 2,000 Chinese scratched out a living in Mokelumne Hill. But a raging fire wiped out their shacks, their washhouses, their Joss House, and most of an adobe building that was an auction room for selling Chinese slave girls.

But when the gold frenzy began to decline, so did the size and prominence of the town. There is little left of the glory that was once Mokelumne Hill...the riotous spirit that made it the wildest of mining camps...the cosmopolitan air that gave it a theater where the miners could watch Shakespearean drama (with female roles played by the more genteel of the men).

MOKELUMNE HILL TODAY

George Leger came to Mokelumne Hill from Germany in 1851 and set up a beer parlor. When it was wiped out by fire a year later, he decided to expand and build a one-story hotel adjoining the Courthouse (handy if County officers got thirsty). Like everything else in Mokelumne Hill in those prosperous years, the hotel thrived. In fact, when the County seat was moved to San Andreas and the Courthouse became available, George Leger saw Opportunity knocking. He bought the defunct building, opened up the thick stone walls, and built a passageway to the new and grand Hotel de L'Europe...most elegant and luxurious hotel in the diggings, meeting place of the rich and famous from the continent and abroad.

It's had a fire or two since then, and several ownership changes over the years. But it's still the same opulent hostelry, dominating Main Street with its canary-yellow exterior, its pillared porch and balconies. And it's still the gathering place for the elite.

Now picturesque, pleasant and sleepy, Mokelumne Hill features winding streets, rhyolite tuff buildings, and picturesque ruins. The Odd Fellows Lodge, still extant, was built in two stages. The two lower floors went up in 1854, the upper story was added seven years later. The Congregational Church is the oldest of that denomination in the state, perched high on a hill overlooking the town. On another hill above the town is the battlefield called French Hill, where Americans stormed the French miners and taught them that patriotism (for France) didn't pay.

A better class of miner's cabin, with its large fireplace for cooking and heating. The floor was the bare ground. Doors and glass windows were almost unknown.

JACKSON, WHERE MINES RUN DEEP

Unlike other towns along the foothills, Jackson didn't spring to life full-blown by the act of some prospector digging in the dirt and coming up with a pocket full of gold-bearing rocks.

In its earlier stages it was an unmarked spot on the landscape called Bottileas (Spanish for Bottles), a stopover for teamsters who liked to take advantage of a fine freshwater spring there. As time went on, the waterhole was easily identifiable by the accumulation of empty bottles tossed aside when refreshment time was over.

The gold was there, though, and Jackson was destined to become a vital center for quartz mining. It prospered long after the boomtowns had faded and were on their way to ghosthood.

By 1850, the town had grown, the litter had been cleaned up, and the name was changed to Jackson.

Jackson was then a part of Calaveras County, but itching to break loose and form a separate county. By 1853 strong sentiment had turned to fever, and several ambitious towns asserted they were willing to accept the responsibility (and financial benefits) of being county seat. Volcano claimed priority as "fastest-growing," but its detractors said it was built in a hole no one could get out of. Sutter Creek filed claim to the honor on the basis of being "the town par excellence where no dance houses or kindred institutions were likely to demoralize public officers" (a sly dig at Mokelumne Hill). Jackson, which had once been Calaveras County seat, rested on Experience.

In spite of some election shenanigans (not uncommon for the times) in which ballots were all opened in advance by Mok Hill officials, the new Amador County became a reality, and Jackson won the county seat.

In 1850 a young man named Andrew Kennedy discovered his gold on a hill overlooking the growing town in the hollow below. It was to become one of the most famous mines in America, for it revolutionized mining process, proving that deep mining was not only possible, but profitable. Its shaft finally poked through the earth to a depth of 4,600 feet, with 150 miles of tunnel spreading out like searching fingers through the surrounding terrain. To cope with flooding at the lower levels, 75,000 gallons of water were pumped out every 24 hours.

Another deep mine that proved profitable was the Argonaut west of town. But during its course it suffered what was perhaps the greatest mining tragedy in California history. Fire, the great fear that spooks underground miners, broke out in the lower depths, and 47 men were trapped below. They died from poisonous gases; but before the end one of them found strength to trace a final message on the slate wall, "Gas too strong 3 a.m."

Another famous miner was Madame Pantaloons, who startled the populace by working her mine wearing men's pants, shirt, and boots at a time when it was simply not done. The Madame did all right, though. She pulled out one hundred thousand dollars before she sold her mine.

JACKSON TODAY

Jackson is unusual for an ex-mining town in that its population of approximately 2,000 has remained constant over its hundred-odd years. Many of its old buildings are preserved, though they may be camouflaged behind latter-day plaster and paint.

The Courthouse is the original one, opened with such impressive ceremony in 1854, when a procession was formed to march through town and take possession. First in the parade was the band, consisting of a cracked drum and asthmatic clarinet, then the firemen in red shirts, followed by a contingent of judges, the District Attorney, the County Clerk and Treasurer...and upon their heels, the general citizenry. Judge Gordon made a splendid speech complimenting the citizens on their liberality. And in a burst of enthusiasm several saloon owners invited officials and citizenry alike to partake of their hospitality. On that generous note, the procession reformed and marched down the street to accept the proffered hospitality.

The most photographed, etched, sketched and painted mining item in the Mother Lode country is the Kennedy tailing wheel, 68 feet in diameter, built in 1912 to take tailings from the Kennedy mine and dump it into a dam behind Jackson.

The rambunctious spirit of Gold Rush times lingered in Jackson longer than in most towns. A rebirth of gambling is still under consideration as a possible source of civic funding.

And the bordellos weren't closed down until 1956. To commemorate the occasion, townsfolk put up a bronze historical marker which reads, "World's oldest profession flourished fifty yards east of this plaque for many years until this most perfect example of free enterprise was padlocked by unsympathetic politicians."

SUTTER CREEK, 1854

SERENE SUTTER CREEK

When John Sutter at last realized that Fate had intervened in his neat plans, that no wages on earth could keep men lumbering and tanning hides when gold lay all about, he decided to join in the madness and find some gold of his own. He loaded wagons with supplies, and left with a work crew of a hundred Indians and fifty Hawaiian servants. After a brief stop ten miles above the Fort, where he found conditions too crowded to suit him ("my people made too many acquaintances"), he headed south and set up a mining enterprise on the site now known as Sutter Creek.

Things didn't go well with him there, either. "I located the camp on Sutter creek, and thought I should be there alone. The work was going on well for a while, until three or four traveling grog shops surrounded me. Then, of course, the gold was taken to these places for drinking, gambling, etc., and the following day they were sick and unable to work. I found that it was high time to quit this kind of business and lose no more time and money. This whole expedition proved to be a heavy loss to me."

It was Sutter's last attempt at mining.

In fact, Sutter Creek didn't gain its first success as a mining camp so much as a supply center for miners. Nevertheless, a young man named Leland Stanford got his start toward the fortune he would later amass, in a Sutter Creek mining venture. Stanford was a petty merchant in Sacramento at the time, and had picked up a share in the Lincoln mine as a substitute for cash in payment of a debt. He was discouraged at prospects of the mine and tried to sell out his share for $5,000, but was talked out of it. Later he sold his interest for $400,000, enough capital to make him a railroad magnate.

When John Sutter decided to join the rush for riches in late summer 1848, he gave his name to the mining camp now known as the town of Sutter Creek.

Placer gold is not inexhaustible. Even the richest dry diggings may be washed down to nothing, for gold does not renew itself, and the tens of thousands of miners who came early combed out the biggest fortunes. Men surged restlessly up and down the foothills, looking for new diggings, fresh rivers. More than one decided that California's gold hills were done for.

The lucky towns, the ones that survived, were the quartz mining towns. But quartz mining is expensive. It's a business of machinery, of drilling and blasting and stamping. It takes capital and plenty of it, and even for those who invested, heartbreaking disappointment.

Quartz leads were uncovered in Sutter Creek as early as 1851. But the town didn't boom until Alvinza Hayward was daring enough to risk the capital it takes to develop hardrock mining.

And Hetty Green, owner of Central Eureka became one of the richest women in the world.

Hayward fared well, too. He reportedly received an income of $50,000 a month from his mining interest.

SUTTER CREEK TODAY

Sutter Creek is a proper and genteel town, built astride 500 miles of mine tunnels. Merchants of the 1860s went in heavily for second-story balconies, which still overhang main street and give the town an uncommonly elegant air not always visible in gold rush towns.

An unhurried pace pervades the community, and it is hard to imagine that once this peaceful town was racked with the din of one hundred stamp mills pounding out gold ore. Those were lusty days, filled with the raucous laughter of rough miners, echoing from the 13 saloons that lined Main Street.

Today Sutter Creek visitors can browse through a townful of antique shops, read the footnotes to history that are posted on ancient buildings, or pick up a copy of the self-guided walking tour sold in local shops. It offers an easy stroll past prim New England-style homes and old-fashioned gardens. Zinnias and nasturtiums bloom in front yards, and tomatoes hang from vines in back yards.

There's a house on Spanish Street, a gracious place of spacious lawns and a giant magnolia tree, which was once the home of R. C. Downs, superintendent of Leland Stanford's mine. Built in the Maine-style that seems to be the pervading architecture of the town, it is now almost exactly as it was in 1873 when it was built.

The Methodist Church dates to 1852. The IOOF Hall and Masonic Hall were built in 1859.

At 31 Eureka Street, two blocks east of Main, is Knight's Foundry, the only water-powered foundry in the United States. Water originates in the headwaters of the Mokelumne River, comes to Sutter Creek by ditch and pipe, drops down to drive the cupped turbines. It has turned out metals for miners (and others) since 1873, and is now a designated historical landmark.

The three-story building on Main Street, between Fifield and Spanish streets, began life as the American Exchange Hotel in 1859. The third floor with its metal Mansard roof and ornate dormers, was added in the 1890s.

OFF THE BEATEN PATH

PLYMOUTH

Very little is known of the early history of Plymouth, except that a small settlement near the lower end of town was once called Pokerville.

One of the early settlers, a man with the unusual name of Green Aden - and later the Hoopers, father and son - came in search of quartz gold. But the mines never amounted to much until 1873 when they were bought up by Alvinza Hayward, D. O. Mills & Co.

Like all early gold towns, Plymouth was racked by fires. The first started in a stable, and in no time at all leveled the town. But villagers made a quick rebound, and before long the town could boast 22 saloons and a fine racetrack on the edge of town (present site of Amador County fairgrounds). Prosperity was the order of the day, with 150 men on the mine payroll and an 80-stamp mill operated by water power.

Fire erased most of Plymouth's early buildings, but the old China Store with its heavy iron fire doors, remains from a time when Plymouth's Chinese population may have outnumbered Caucasians.

But bad luck was waiting in the wings. A fire broke out in the mines that smouldered for four months before it was finally doused. It was a mortal blow to the town. Not until 1911 was the mine rebuilt, this time by a mining expert from London with the help of a dashing Italian prince named Galesio Caetani - mining engineer, stateman, ambassador, and one of the most unusual characters to appear on the California mining scene.

By 1947, mining came to an end in Plymouth, as in much of the Mother Lode country. Today Plymouth is a trading center for some rich agricultural land and the vineyards that stretch out into the Shenandoah Valley.

Still, reminders of its golden days remain in a few aging buildings around town, and in the tilting head frame of a mine that once produced $13 million in gold.

AMADOR CITY

Amador City takes its name from a rancher, Jose Amador, who did a little mining in the vicinity at the start of the Gold Rush. But Jose wasn't satisfied with results, and moved on. Three years later, four ministers-turned-miners made the first quartz discovery in the region in a claim that came to be known as Minister's Gulch. The preachers prospected for gold on weekdays and for men's souls on Sundays.

The Keystone Mine, whose rusty head frame still looks down on the town, was one of the richest mines in California. The Mine House, built later, was headquarters. Today it has been turned into an inn, the bedrooms named to suit their original use - Vault, Assay, Retort -all furnished in the style of times when the mine was a target for bandits.

Also of interest: The Imperial Hotel, an imposing two-story brick structure with iron doors and shutters, and the Amador Hotel (dating back to 1856), which is now a restaurant. The historic Torres Hall building now houses the Amador Winery.

The Wells Fargo office, with its worn plank floor concealing a vault beneath it, is still intact after 112 years.

AND MORE...

FIDDLETOWN - A visitor to the town in the 1860s complained there wasn't a single fiddler in town to play for dances.

There was once a large Chinese population, and the ruins of the fort they built to protect themselves against Mexican intruders, can still be found.

RAILROAD FLAT - This may be the oldest settlement in the region, established in 1847 by Mexicans. It has no railroad. Until 1866 the settlement was called Independence, but names were invented on slight provocation, and when a man riding through town on a horse saw a man pulling an ore cart on rails laid by miners, he dubbed it Railroad Flat.

SHEEP RANCH - Originally a sheep ranch, a town blossomed when gold was discovered in the sheep corral. Five mines were operating, one bought in 1875 by George Hearst for $108,000.

SONORA, A MEXICAN CAMP

"I had never seen a more beautiful, a more romantic spot, than Sonora," said William Perkins, a Canadian who came to Sonora in the Spring of 1849. "On Saturdays and Sundays, the camp used to wear, night and day, an almost magic appearance. Lights shone from gaily decorated houses, all of them with their fronts open to the streets, and the streets themselves strewn with lighted tapers."

It was Mexicans who first settled along the southern strip of the Sierra foothills and found gold in abundance. They named the settlement Sonora, after their hometown province in Mexico.

But their charming way of life, as described by Perkins (who stayed on and became a storekeeper) wasn't destined to last. It changed from paradise to problems when Americans drifted down from northern diggings.

Racial tolerance was never notable in the diggings. The average Yankee miner, educated or not, distrusted and disliked "greasers" (that term was actually written into some laws), by which he meant anybody from south of the Rio Grande. Distaste was even more pronounced when the Mexicans or Chilenos, who were experienced in the skills of mining, did better than the greenhorn American.

This preoccupation with intolerance led, in 1850, to a Foreign Miners' Tax Law which imposed a fee of $20 a month on all miners of foreign birth.

By September, with three-fourths of the population deserting, Sonora became a dead town and lapsed into hard times. Even the Sonora Herald had to suspend for lack of patronage. But the hated tax was repealed in 1851, and Mexicans started wandering back to the gold fields.

In Sonora, racial resentment bordered on the fanatical. Suspicions and rumors of wrongdoing were rampant. Outbursts between camps were frequent. It finally led to armed confrontation. The Mexicans, of course, were in a state of intense ferment over the tax. When word was brought to the American mining camps that the Mexican flag had been raised, all hell broke loose. Within an hour, every miner in the area rallied, and was marching on the offenders. Hot tempers were further inflamed by the fact it was a hot day necessitating several stops at grog shops along the way. As they proceeded, new intelligence was passed along that the "greasers" were armed and preparing for assault.

When the marchers reached the Mexican camp, they were surprised to see its inhabitants "very quietly seated in front of their brush hovels, playing monte and other games, as if nothing unusual had transpired."

The Mexicans, of course, were no less surprised to see a column of armed men advancing. Thoroughly frightened, they decided to pack their burros and leave.

Sonora was the site of some spectacular gold finds, especially during late 1848. Finds amounting to hundreds and even thousands of dollars, were too common to excite comment, and the labor of a single week often produced enough to carry some fortunate miner to his home in the East. Such news spread magically in Gold Country, and prospectors poured in to share the good luck.

In fact, travel was reported to be so constant that "the campfires on the trail from Stockton to Sonora were near enough together to show the traveller his way."

As a result of this influx, prices skyrocketed. Everything sold at a uniform $3 a pound, except salt pork which was $8. Meanwhile, gold devaluated to $8 an ounce in coin ($16 in trade).

Other problems plagued the diggings. An outbreak of scurvy, brought on by a diet of salted provisions, afflicted half the residents. A special hospital was built to treat the sick with lime juice ($5 a bottle) and raw potatoes ($1.50 per lb.).

One of the most popular Sunday afternoon entertainments for miners was the bull-and-bear fight. Reported the Sonora Herald: "A fantastically dressed Mexican clown, preceded by a band of shockingly bad music, parades the streets, notifying the citizens of a fight about to come off.

Bear and bull fighting, a favorite Sunday afternoon diversion for miners, was certainly not for the fainthearted.

A 600-lb. grizzly bear was enclosed in a pen, chained either to a post or his opponent, a mean bull twice his size. If they didn't take unkindly enough to one another on initial meeting, the promoters got up a little spirit by goading them with spears. It didn't much matter to the spectators whether the bear, with his sharp teeth and powerful jaws, got to the bull's neck first - or the bull, with superior weight and sharp horns, gored the bear. Blood was the object.

Sometimes the spectators themselves became part of the sport. In a Sonora arena, jammed with 2,000 spectators, a wounded bull jumped the fence and ran wild through the crowd, goring one man to death and trampling several others.

Meanwhile, another incident was taking place inside the arena. The promoter decided to throw some water on the exhausted bear, and was grabbed by the animal who commenced to chew on his leg. Several volleys of pistol shots killed the bear, but not in time to save his victim.

An attempt was made to discourage this cruel sport in 1856 by imposing a $25 licensing fee (not much of a deterrent). But it wasn't until 1905 that it was outlawed altogether.

But by 1854 Sonora had turned to more sedate family life. The Sonora Herald approved, "Now, instead of the bull-and-bear fights on this sacred day, troops of rosy-faced, quiet, orderly children are seen returning from Sunday school. And where men from the surrounding camps once quarreled, fought, drank, swore, and squandered their hard-earned means at the gambling table or low brothel, now well-dressed men and women are on their way to church.

"And what has caused this great change in public sentiment?" the editor inquires. "The presence of woman, virtuous, pure, sympathizing woman, the great controller of public opinion, without whom society is dull and existence a blank."

SONORA TODAY

A most historic and charming structure in town is the brick-red frame St. James' Episcopal Church (built in 1860) at the north end of Washington Street. Across the street is another red building, the home in early Glory Days of S. Bradford (of the Mayflower Bradfords), who brought lumber around the Horn and decorated it with gingerbread trim.

For the true spirit of early Mother Lode, though, nothing comes closer to the old trading post saloon of early mining days than Servente's grocery store in the middle of town. It's divided in half by a sign hung from the ceiling which reads "no minors"...the only combination grocery store and barroom in the state. Women have only recently been allowed.

The oldest house in Sonora now is the Gunn House, built in 1850 by Dr. Gunn, a pioneer whose name is on virtually every civic document of early days. Today it has been expanded into an extremely comfortable hostelry, decorated with antiques that would make Dr. Gunn feel right at home.

The back streets of Sonora are more reminiscent of old times than downtown.

Still and all, there are few ghosts left in Sonora of those rip-roaring days when a good, bloody bull-and-bear fight was a usual way to celebrate the Sabbath.

COLUMBIA: A GEM

The plot of ground that eventually became Columbia, with incredibly rich diggings, wasn't explored until 1850, though it was in the middle of a mining area being worked energetically by both Americans and Mexicans. Perhaps it had been bypassed because there was no river running nearby, and water is essential to placer mining.

The first to start puttering in the gravel were Mexicans who had been tossed out of the Sonora diggings and had wandered over the hills in search of new lucrative soil. With winter rains providing a stream to work in, they had results beyond expectations.

Their good fortune didn't remain exclusive very long. In March, Dr. Thaddeus Hildreth and a handful of prospectors came upon the scene, stuck a shovel into Kennebec Hill, and almost instantly gathered thirty pounds of nuggets - and thereby set off another stampede to the new diggings. Before a month had passed, a tent-and-shanty town called Hildreth's Diggings had been created, and 5,000 miners, frantically digging and washing the rich, red earth, called it home.

The town was destined for two decades of glory - ten years of roaring life, and ten years of trying desperately to believe the gold would never be exhausted.

That first year came close to being its last. When the runoff water from spring thaws dried up in the gulches, there was no way to work the dirt. The population rapidly fell off until not a dozen men remained, making their daily beans by hauling dirt a long distance to water. The answer was a system of ditches and races and flumes and reservoirs, developed the following April by the newly formed Tuolumne Water Company, and later expanded at a cost of a cool two million dollars.

With that technicality out of the way, the rude mining camp turned into a tumultuous city of 20,000. Before boom turned to bust, Columbia's topsoil gave up almost $90 million in gold, and Columbia reveled in booming prosperity.

A couple of disastrous fires put an end to canvas and wood, and a new main street was created, a graceful blend of red brick and wrought iron, containing such sterling business enterprises as 143 gambling palaces, 30 saloons, a dozen fandango parlors...and, on the cultural side, two theaters (one of them Chinese, with 40 Oriental actors), four banks, eight hotels, and a branch of the Sons of Temperance. The four-mile road from Columbia to Sonora was lined solid with miners' shanties.

One of the four banks belonged to Darius Ogden Mills, who picked up a little experience in the banking business before going on to the Big Time controlling the destiny of Virginia City.

Next door to the Mills bank, Wells Fargo painstakingly weighed out something like $55 million in gold over the years, an ounce at a time, before the whole whoop-de-doo ended and there was no more gold to weigh. So precise were the scales, the miners claimed, that "they could show the weight of a pencil mark on paper."

After the town's second disastrous fire, citizens wearied of replacing wooden buildings and set to work organizing a volunteer fire department. A committee was dispatched to San Francisco to buy an engine, and struck a fine bargain with a small, fancifully decorated handpumper which had been destined for Tahiti but was stranded on a ship in the Bay, abandoned by sailors who thought gold was more important than seeing the world.

The lads of the Volunteer Fire Department were among the most respected men in town, present at every parade and public function. They were a chivalrous lot, too. Word got around that Big Annie, keeper of a back street fandango parlor, had bumped into the town's prim school mistress, forcing her into a dusty road. The teacher delicately lifted her skirt, and Annie guffawed and made fun of the teacher's legs. That night the volunteer fire department, affronted by the indignity, wheeled its apparatus up to Annie's shabby establishment and spewed forth a powerful stream of water, washing the old girl out of the building (and out of town).

Miners were ever eager for entertainment and diversion. When travelling troupes of actors started making the circuit of mining towns, every man went to see them. Enthusiastic, red-shirted miners escorted the actors to and from the theater, even carried their effusive good wishes into the privacy of dressing rooms.

One of the most popular troupes was the Chapman Family. When they played Columbia, the miners showed their appreciation by tossing buckskin purses, each containing what the generous miners thought a proper testimonial, until the stage was covered. Then a procession of over a thousand miners acted as escort on the Chapman's journey to Sonora, where they presented a comedy in three acts, "The Serious Family," followed by dancing and singing.

By 1860 the easily mined placer gold had all been scraped up and sifted. Columbia faded as fast as it had mushroomed. Population plummeted to 500. The handsome buildings were vacated, and gold-hungry prospectors tore them down to see if there might be an undiscovered cache of nuggets still in the foundation dirt.

COLUMBIA TODAY

Columbia has charm. In summer the bees hum in the spreading boughs of the ailanthus, the Trees of Heaven planted by the Chinese who followed after the white man to wash the gold remnants from the tailings.

Columbia has been a State Historical Park since 1945, and is probably the best preserved gold rush town in the foothills.

The once lusty city never really died and turned into a ghost; it drowsed peacefully in the Sierra foothills, still alive but far removed from the soon-to-be-established paths of railroads and highways.

The 1861 schoolhouse on the hill was saved by the schoolchildren of California, who collected nickels and dimes to save it from decay. The cemetery nearby is the town's second graveyard. The first was torn up when gold was discovered there.

The Fallon House hotel-theater was built shortly after the fire of 1857. The miner was no savage, though he dressed roughly when at work. Miners in baggy Levis watched Edwin Booth play Richard III, and cheered Lola Montez when she performed her famous Spider Dance "in perfect rhythm to the clicking of castanets." (One would surely hope so!)

One of the major entertainment attractions is the eight-week summer repertory season at the Fallon Theater, when college students from the University of the Pacific perform in modern drama.

The City Hotel (originally the What Cheer House) is a training center for Columbia Junior College's restaurant management program. The menu is French and beautiful.

According to legend, one of Columbia's early restaurants had a French cook named Antoine who achieved a fame of sorts from a dish he once concocted. He stewed and seasoned a cat so well that no one could tell it from rabbit. He won a $50 bet with his unique cooking ability - though he later lost some of his steady customers when the story leaked out.

A century has not diminished Columbia's charm. Though the streets now are filled with throngs of tourists instead of miners, it remains the best surviving collection of the Gold Rush era.

COARSEGOLD

When Mexican miners started prospecting an arroyo at the southern end of the gold chain, they named it Oso Grosso, Castilian for "coarse gold." Disdaining the fine surface gold, they dug down to bedrock and scraped until they found gold in round grains of several ounces.

The size of the nuggets foretold the future of this mining town; it became the center of profitable quartz mining.

In 1853 four men from Texas, new in town, were persuaded by "old hands" to work a supposedly worthless hill mine. They struck a rich vein and acquired a fortune.

Little remains of the old Coarsegold, except a pumphouse bearing the date 1852 on its cornerstone.

MARIPOSA, AN UNTAMED LAND

The name Mariposa (Spanish for butterfly) was first applied to a small creek discovered by some caballeros on a hunting foray in 1806.

But until the 1849 Gold Discovery the entire region was virtually unknown to white men. It was the domain of numerous Indian tribes, mostly hostile, all expert with bow and arrow.

The first step in improving relations with the Indians was made by Major James Savage who established a log trading post on the south fork of the Merced River. He married a number of squaws from various tribes, for protection and influence.

Other pioneers weren't so fortunate.

An exploring party from San Miguel was massacred in March 1849; that same month another party, working Burns Creek below Mariposa, was driven out by Indian attacks.

Nevertheless, in early 1850 when Charles Pancoast arrived in the Mariposa diggings, he found a small trading post and a line of muddy holes and rusty picks and shovels along the bottom of the ravine. Max, who ran the trading post, advanced him $300 in supplies on credit (at gouging prices), enabling Pancoast to build a rocker and get started.

It was the rough beginning of a permanent camp. Soon afterward, a wagon train of fifty men arrived, including storekeepers, mechanics, miners, and gamblers. They surveyed the ground and staked out streets.

Mariposa was a town.

Initially the town of Agua Fria (now gone) was the county seat of the sprawling Mariposa County, which covered an area from Tuolumne to Los Angeles Pueblo, and from the Coast range to the Territory of Utah (now Nevada).

While the County government was being conducted from the log-cabin Courthouse in Agua Fria, Joseph Marr became the Treasurer. It was his custom to go from diggings to diggings on horseback collecting taxes, which he would bring back to his office and secrete the funds as best he could with no safe in which to keep collections.

One day a terrific storm arose and, in crossing a swollen stream, he and his horse were drowned. No trace of the County funds was ever found, although he was known to have had 300 of the $50 Mt. Ophir gold slugs the day previous. No one knows that this gold was ever found. It may still be buried in the vicinity of the first Courthouse.

- Historian Newell Chamberlain

The county seat was transferred to Mariposa in 1852, and within two years Mariposa had progressed from a tent hamlet to a city of several thousand. It had a more substantial air than most Mother Lode towns, because quartz mines (which could be worked year-round) brought in men with families. The town wasn't dependent on the vagaries of placer mining.

John Fremont - the dashing, the flamboyant, the "pathfinder" of a way West - found California greatly to his liking. In 1847 he resigned his Army post and decided to settle down near San Francisco Bay. He sent $3,000 to his friend, the American consul of Monterey, and asked him to buy a ranch near San Jose. What his friend bought him for $3,000 was a mammoth floating Mexican grant of 44,000 acres in what was then a wild and worthless region. Fremont was furious, and started on foot to California to get his $3,000 back. Along the way, he learned that gold had been discovered in the Sierra foothills.

With this change of situation, Fremont took a second look at his $3,000 purchase and decided to have it surveyed. He floated his grant to include the Mother Lode gold belt from Mariposa to the Merced River. It was the beginning of years of strife and costly litigation.

Into this tense situation, Fremont brought his society wife, his three children, and some friends, to turn wilderness into home. While the explorer (now mine owner) struggled with his rancho and its legal entanglements, Jessie and the others made up a gay and carefree company, riding horseback by day, holding sprightly conversation in the evenings. For the cultivated Jessie, it was an adventurous contrast to the drawing rooms of Washington.

It was in Mariposa that mining first turned from placer diggings to quartz mining. In the beginning, Fremont worked his rich placers by grubstaking Mexican miners. As they dug into the rich leads uncovered at grass roots, they followed a golden path to the quartz location that was the heart of the Mother Lode.

His extravagant and wasteful methods of mining were attacked by the press then, and by historians since.

Nevertheless, Fremont imported the first stamp mill machinery and did much for the development of Mariposa County, while himself living in splendor at his Bear Valley home (the "White House"). In 1860 he sold his grant for six million dollars. But it didn't save him from the financial ruin his years of litigation had cost him. After his wealth was gone, Jessie took to writing magazine articles.

MARIPOSA TODAY

One of the most handsome Gold Rush structures in the entire state is the charming, New England style Courthouse in Mariposa. It was built in 1854 from lumber whipsawed from the neighboring forests. The framework was fitted together with mortise and tenon joints, and held in place with wooden pegs. Finished lumber was hand-planed. But it is the English-made clock, in its high clock tower, that elevates this Courthouse above all others.

Some of Fremont's legal problems were settled here, one way or another. The Judge's bench is the original, and the tables and seats are the same ones used by Fremont, by scores of early miners, and a long procession of attorneys.

Other structures of historic interest in town include the old Trabucco Store, the Odd Fellows Hall, and St. Joseph's Catholic Church.

Mariposa is, of course, a gateway to Yosemite National Park. It was in March 1851 that Major Savage first penetrated this canyon, an Indian stronghold. The Indians boasted that if white men tried to enter it they would be corralled like mules. One member of the expedition, in spite of the dangers that surrounded him, was awestruck by what he saw...

"The grandeur of the scene was but softened by the haze that hung over the valley, light as gossamer, and by the clouds which partially dimmed the higher cliffs and mountains. This obscurity of vision but increased the awe with which I beheld it, and as I looked, a peculiar exalted sensation seemed to fill my whole being and I found my eyes in tears with emotion."

Perhaps visitors today feel much the same.

Refreshment time at the National Hotel's saloon in Jamestown, 1895.

JAMESTOWN

In August 1848, a party of Philadelphians under the leadership of a militant clergyman, Rev. James Woods, started panning a creek a mile south of present-day Jamestown, and in spite of their haphazard methods were soon taking out $300 a day, using little more than a jack knife.

Two of the party, a San Francisco lawyer named Colonel James and a man called George, worked their way upstream a mile or so, and since they never seemed to get along with one another, George was on one side of the stream and the Colonel on the other. Both had been followed by their cronies, and in time two separate settlements formed --George's town and Jim's town.

But George's popularity soon dwindled, and his followers moved across the stream to Jim's town -- Jamestown today.

Alas, Colonel James was not known for his scruples, either, and his disgruntled followers finally forced him out of the camp. In fact, his high-handedness had incurred the ill will of his followers to such an extent that on his departure the name of the town was changed, out of revenge, to American Camp. But the name Jamestown was too firmly fixed, and after a time both the feud and the new name were forgotten.

The placer mines of Jamestown eventually yielded $3 million in gold. Lode mines were active from the 1860s on. From 1890 until World War I, lode mining was a major industry and the town grew to a population of 6,000. By the turn of the century, more than 300 stamps were "dropping" in various mills in the district.

In 1897 the Sierra Railroad was built to connect the mines of the Mother Lode with freight centers in the San Joaquin Valley.

Originally, the line set out from Oakdale, to the somewhat gloomy predictions that tracks would never get 20 miles farther. Nevertheless, by summer the Sierra had reached Jamestown. Three years later it had reached Tuolumne City, headquarters of the West Side Lumber Company. Sierra's "Old Number Three" and other rolling stock has been featured in movies and on T.V., notably in High Noon, Dodge City, Duel in the Sun, Petticoat Junction, and Little House on the Prairie.

DOWNIEVILLE, TINCUP TOWN

The gold fever that burned with such intensity from Coloma southward, also found its way north, moving like some pestilential wave of fortune along the canyons of the Yuba.

North from Auburn, the scenery changes dramatically. The yellow oak-studded foothills climb into green mountains, through a high country of thick pine forests, jagged snow-streaked buttes, and steep-walled canyons.

Into this overwhelming country in 1849 came William Downie, a 30-year-old Scot.

As early as 1848, wandering miners had tested their pans in the Yuba River and found especially rich diggings wherever the river had been diverted, leaving sand bars. At Rose's Bar, Downie first joined forces with Jim Rose, another Scot, then he moved upriver to Bullard's Bar. Here he observed that the miners who consistently paid for provisions with the largest lumps of gold were working further up the Yuba. He immediately formed a party of prospectors and led them upriver.

A miner at Foster's Bar told him it was too late in the season to travel into such rough country, but Downie was determined. One night the men caught a salmon and boiled it; next morning there was gold in the cook pot!

So there, in the fork of two rivers, the men mined, even in winter, finding gold in abundance. Their luck got better every day, from 17 ounces to 24, to 29, to 40 ounces a day. They built a cabin in December, and sent two of the men downriver for provisions (for which Downie paid $3900 - $2 a pound for everything). And in spite of 40 miles of dangerous mountain trails, the miners flocked in to join them. It was cold, and it snowed. Tents collapsed, and no food could be freighted over the hills. But gold was there.

Downie was a generous, good-hearted soul. When the storekeeper became ill, it was Downie who nursed him back to health. When he was well again, storekeeper Slater offered to return Downie's favor by taking his gold down to Sacramento, where he said they were paying $22 an ounce instead of the standard $16. When this word spread around camp, all the men decided to get in on this good deal, so that when Slater left he had $25,000 worth of gold on him, including some gold that Downie had sent along as a gift for Mrs. Slater, by way of appreciation.

Slater was never seen in the digs again. But Downie heard about him indirectly. A latecomer to the diggings said he had met Slater in Panama, and he had recommended that he look up Downie, "one of the best fellows in the world, ready to do all in his power to assist a stranger."

In spite of the fact that Downieville (then known as The Forks) was 75 miles from the main source of supplies, that food was murderously expensive, and that the streams were icy cold to work in, the town grew to 5,000 within two years. It became known as the town of Tincup Diggings, since a full tin cup was about an average day's wages.

Like all gold towns, The Forks had its incidents of injustice. One awful morning they hanged Juanita, a pretty dance-hall girl. Downie described her: "She was of the Spanish-Mexican mixture, proud and self-possessed, her bearing graceful, almost majestic. She was, in the miners' parlance, well put up." On a drunken Fourth of July night, a man named Cannon staggered into her cabin, left, but came back the next day. Juanita put a knife into him.

A lynch court promptly sentenced her to hang. Juanita mounted the scaffold beside the river, "apparently unmoved, she seemed quite satisfied to abide by the verdict." She adjusted the noose around her neck, straightened her skirt, called out, "Adios, Senors," and leaped from the scaffold into eternity.

Legend has it that William Downie, who had by now elevated himself to the rank of Major, offered the town a mining pan full of gold if they'd change the town's name from The Forks to Downieville. History doesn't record whether the town got the gold, but it is no longer called The Forks.

OTHER TREASURES

SIERRA CITY - Between Downieville and Sierra City, the canyon walls grow higher and steeper. The river below flashes green and white through the darkness of the pines. At a final high turn, the panorama opens onto Sierra City, somewhat overshadowed by the magnificence of its own setting.

Philo Haven and Joseph Zumwalt stopped here to mine in 1850, in a favorite fishing ground of the Indians. But it was more quartz country than placer country, and not until quartz mining came of age did Sierra City blossom.

When it did, it was riotous.

It was here that the noted and notorious miners' fraternal order, E Clampus Vitus, got its start. Every town in the Mother Lode had an IOOF building. The Clampers thought the membership too tame. So they invented E. Clampus Vitus, the greatest practical joke ever conceived to make light of the hardships and miseries of the diggings. The members were largely devoted to hilarity and hard drinking, although a more worthy purpose was stated to be "taking care of widows and orphans -especially widows." But their boisterous ceremonies, washed in a wave of whiskey, were hilarious, and ridiculed every stuffy and pompous ceremony held sacred by other organizations.

ALLEGHANY - The drive alone is worth the trip. As you climb higher and higher, you can look out over the backbone of the Sierra Nevada. Many of the old wooden houses still cling to the steep sides of Kanaka Canyon.

The town called You Bet got its name when saloon-keeper Lazarus Bard enlisted the help of a couple of his "regulars" to find a suitable name for the settlement that had grown up around his grog shop. While they employed their brains in this service, he poured free whiskey. Realizing the tenuous nature of their supply, the men were careful to suggest only names that would be objectionable. But after a few days, their deliberations were becoming difficult. Then they noticed that the expression "you bet" was a great favorite of the barkeep, so they offered that as a possible name. To their surprise, it met with favor and was adopted, and their free whiskey came to an end.

MALAKOFF DIGGINS - They tore down mountains to get to the gold. It was the biggest hydraulic mine in the world.

Hydraulic mining required enormous amounts of water, which was brought in through elaborate flumes, then shot through a monitor (a long iron tube like a fire hose nozzle, sometimes eight inches in diameter), in a jet stream that could kill a man a hundred feet away. Gold-bearing quartz was washed down into a drain tunnel lined with sluice boxes. Once a month the miners went through the tunnel to collect the gold. As more gold was unearthed, the pits became enormous.

Today the enormous scars at Malakoff are preserved in a state historic park. The passing years have softened the ugly erosion, and the place resembles a miniature Bryce Canyon.

NORTH SAN JUAN - Shells of ancient stone-and-brick buildings lie in half-ruin, ghosts of a time when the town rang with the laughter of men who mined San Juan Ridge.

Its most impressive structure is a charming white New England style Methodist church on a hillock above the town.

ROUGH AND READY - This once feisty town is now but a dwindling relic of early days when it seceded from the Union and declared itself a free and independent state. The strange chain of events was put into motion in 1850, when residents of the then bustling gold rush town grew fed up with high taxes and too much interference from the federal government. Col. E. F. Brundage was elected president amid a giant celebration, and the free state of Rough and Ready remained active until the end of the Civil War.

The bold, historic declaration was eventually forgotten, until 1948, when local townspeople applied for a post office. Uncle Sam issued an ultimatum: "Join the United States, or do without a post office."

NEVADA CITY, A LATECOMER

In the autumn of 1849, three mining partners raised "color" in the gravel of Deer Creek, and with supreme optimism immediately set to work notching logs for a cabin. Perhaps the raising of a cabin instead of the usual flimsy tent foretold the substantial nature of the town that would rise there.

Within a month, a ready-made family arrived - a settler named Stamps, his wife, her sister, and several children. The arrival of women in the uninhibited, rough male world of mining camps was no small event, but it was followed almost immediately by the arrival of a miner named Penn, who brought his wife to help work his claim. (The following spring she gave up mining and opened a boarding house.)

Dr. Caldwell moved his trading post up from downriver, giving the diggings, briefly, the name Caldwell's Upper Store. Some miners called it Deer Creek Dry Diggins.

When the gravel slopes were found to be fabulously rich, miners flocked in from a hundred miles up and down the Sierra. They pried out gold by the pound, sometimes using nothing more than a knife. By autumn of 1850 that first log cabin had been multiplied by 250, some 6,000 people populated the hills in varying degrees of permanency. Mr. Stamps had been elected alcalde, and the town was christened Nevada.

The account of 49er Ben Avery describes his arrival in Nevada City in October, 1849: "Arrived at Caldwell's Store, the only trading post on Deer creek at that time. I found it a square canvas shanty, stocked with whiskey, pork, and mouldly biscuits. About a dozen parties were working the bars with dug-out cradles and rawhide hoppers."

Finding good success on a spot slightly upstream, he decided to go back to Mormon Island and get his friends. When he again returned in February, he was aghast at the changes. "To my intense disgust I found my ravine occupied from one end to another by long-haired Missourians. They worked in the stormiest weather, standing in the yellow mud to shovel dirt into cradle; one of them had stretched a canvas awning over the claims. All the other ravines were occupied almost as thickly. Dyer had a log cabin in the midst, where whiskey and brandy were sold. Caldwell's new, or upper store, was on the high bank of the ravine. It appears there had been great discoveries. American Hill was covered with tents and brush houses, a few had put up cabins. At night the tents shone through the pines like great transparencies, and the sound of laughter, shouting, fiddling and singing startled those old primeval solitudes strangely. It was a wild, wonderful scene.

Those adventuresome men who once lined the banks of the golden creek, or squeezed for space on the pocked hillsides of this thriving camp, have been left anonymous by the passage of time, their names written fleetingly on the shifting sands of fortune. But for some, Nevada City was only the beginning of fortune.

Benjamin Avery, an early miner, became U.S. Minister to China.

Herbert Hoover, who came to Nevada City with his engineering degree from Stanford, went on to the Presidency.

George Hearst started the fortune that eventually founded a newspaper empire.

Richard Oglesby, who was one of the camp's pioneers, wrote many years later, when he was governor of Illinois: "There was very little law, but a large amount of good order; no churches, but a great deal of religion; no politics, but a large number of politicians; no offices, and strange to say for my countrymen, no office seekers. Crime was rare, for punishment was certain."

But of perhaps greater fascination at the time was the town's most colorful character, Madame Eleanor Dumont, a lady gambler whose beauty was marred by one flaw - a flaw that earned her the nickname by which she was known throughout California and Nevada: Madame Moustache. (The Madame later died of hemlock in bad, bad Bodie.)

No town among the hundreds in the Sierra foothills suffered greater or more frequent trials by fire and flood, and none survived more tenaciously. In its first year, half the town was wiped out by fire, and rebuilt. Four months later, torrential rains and rampaging streams battered the new buildings into kindling and tossed them down the river, along with the Broad Street bridge.

Four years later, when the town had grown to a thousand houses (and 79 saloons), the worst fire in history occurred. It took just 30 minutes to level every wooden building in the business district, including the town's seven hotels.

One of the strangest of duels occurred one October day in 1851 when George M. Dibble called E. N. Lundy a liar on Broad Street. Lundy took exception to the remark and cursed Dibble in colorful terms, calling him some names that Dibble didn't feel he deserved. As a result, he challenged Lundy to a duel. The meeting, with pistols at 15 paces, occurred at sunrise. At the signal, Lundy fired. "You have fired too soon," Dibble remarked calmly. When his second asked if he were satisfied, he opened his shirt and showed where the bullet had passed through his body. Then, declining aid, he walked away, to die in twenty minutes.

The 1850s were the boom years, when quartz mining brought 15,000 population.

And in 1859 Nevada City became the curtain-raiser for the Comstock Lode drama. It was to J. J. Ott's office that a man named Harrison came riding one day, bearing a sample of some blue clay from the Washoe hills. Ott made test after test, barely able to believe his own incredible results. The despised "blue stuff" that was clogging the miners' rockers proved to be an exceedingly rich silver sulphide assaying at $3,000 a ton silver and another $800 in gold. The news of Ott's assay couldn't be held back. It started the rush to Washoe.

NEVADA CITY TODAY

The hub of commerce was established on the only level spot in the diggings. Steep streets meander from this hollow up into hills where lofty pines poke above rooftops and church spires. It's a hometown kind of place, where history keeps happy company with today.

Nevada City sits on a collection of hills around the Deer Creek Ravine. The hills bear colorful names that give a picture of social and economic strata of life in the early town.

On Potters Hill, paupers were buried in a nondescript plot behind the City Jail.

Aristocracy Hill was named for some genteel Southern lads who came to the mines for wealth - but finding the miners less than couth, they built a splendid home to get away from the dreary life of grubbing.

On Prospect Hill, one of the finest of the old homes, the Red Castle, was built in 1859 for Lorin Williams, socialite and attorney.

Nabob Hill was fashionable territory when Victorian architecture was all the go. Rich mining men and physicians established stately homes there. But even nabobs have their tragedies. Grocer Charles Mulloy, rich and respected, one day put a grim end to his life. No one knew why.

Nevada City's winding streets follow the old foot paths taken by miners who came into town for their whiskey and their beans, then went back to some hole in the hills, or a drafty cabin called home.

One of the most famed buildings in town is the National Hotel, built in 1854 as the National Exchange Hotel. It still wears its original ornate, balconied exterior. Once it was the stomping grounds of Madame Moustache, of Herbert Hoover, and of Stephen Field, who became a Supreme Court Justice. And it was here, also that P.G. & E. was hatched in a contract that brought together two electrical equipment experts and a Cornish miner. The National was the busiest spot in town -headquarters for the stage lines, the telegraph, and for Wells Fargo. And in smoke-filled rooms, mining and commerce magnates closed million-dollar deals.

If the National is the most famous, the Firehouse is the most photographed.

An utterly charming structure trimmed with spindles and icicles, it dates back to 1861 (a little late for most of the fires). There's a museum inside displaying a fine collection of the garb and gear of pioneer times, as well as some artifacts from the ill-fated Donner Party.

GRASS VALLEY, LOLA'S TOWN

At first, Grass Valley was an emigrant's stop. A resting place after a long and dusty journey. A meadow where weary cattle could roam and graze on the lush green grasses.

In the autumn of 1848 a small group emigrating from Oregon stopped here, at Greenhorn Creek, decided to build a rough cabin and spend the winter. A group from Boston lingered, too. They moved farther into the meadow and did some panning. A small store was set up, and the camp was called Boston Ravine. It was the beginning of a small settlement.

Perhaps Boston Ravine would have remained quiet and undistinguished forever if it hadn't been for McKnight. One of McKnight's cows strayed, and when he took out after the bovine he stubbed his toe on an outcropping of quartz. Catching a glitter in the broken rock, he broke it up with a hammer and washed out gold.

Gold in solid rock? It was an unknown possibility to the squatters encamped there. They surveyed the rocky hills all about them, scrambled up the slopes, and began to break off chunks. One man pulverized a rock as big as his head, and washed out five hundred dollars.

The neighboring camps promptly went crazy. They all rushed to Boston Ravine to clamber around the hills and smash rocks with hammers. Every cabin became a miniature quartz mill. But no more five-hundred-dollar boulders were found. There was gold in the rock, all right, but not enough to pay for the work involved.

It was a problem that was to bedevil quartz miners for some time to come.

They tried everything.

Some Mexicans built an arrastra operated by mule power to break up the quartz. Some Germans on Wolf Creek built a quartz mill operated by water power; the stamps were tree trunks shod with iron. One Doctor Rodgers built a furnace smelter, filled it with quartz and firewood and kept up a fire for two days.

All failed.

When the problems were eventually solved, it was with money. Big investment is a requirement of quartz mining. At best, the twisting veins are elusive. They disappear into the rock, are found again. Success is followed by shutdown.

Nevertheless, the town of Grass Valley was growing. By 1851 population had reached 20,000. And the community found it had problems other than quartz mining to solve.

"Gold fever was as contagious as the itch," a gold panner of 1850 wrote in his journal. "If you took it, brimstone and grease would not cure you. The only remedy was for you to go to the mines and try your luck."

The winter of 1852-53 was a harsh one. Heavy rains had turned the road to Sacramento into a knee-high muddy slough. Getting provisions into town became a problem of monumental proportions. Prices tripled. A meeting was called at Beatty's Hotel to consider solutions, and the following hard-line resolution was adopted: "Therefore, be it Resolved, that appealing to High Heaven for justice, we will go to San Francisco and obtain the necessary supplies - peaceably if we can, but forcibly if we must."

The trip never came off. There was no money for travelling expenses.

If it wasn't flood, it was fire.

On a September morning in 1855, fire broke out in the United States Hotel - spread rapidly. Flames licked at tinder dry buildings, dried in the long summer sun. When the crackling had stopped, all that remained were the churches and the temperance hall and the Wells Fargo vault. Before the debris stopped smouldering, the recovery process had begun. In the smoky distance at the west end of town, a frame shanty was seen moving down the hill. Slowly but surely it advanced onto the scene of desolation. In a few moments, the energetic entrepreneur, "Old Block" Delano, had backed it up to the Wells Fargo brick vault and put up a 10-foot scantling board on which was rudely painted, "Wells Fargo & Co. Express Office." Less than eight hours after the cry of fire, "Old Block" stood smiling behind his counter, the ground still warm beneath his feet, "ready to attend to business."

In 1854, Lola Montez bought a house and made Grass Valley the scene of her eccentricities for two years. Long on chutzpah, though short on talent, she arrived in town with a husband, a pet bear, and a suitcase full of low-cut velvet gowns.

Once, as the mistress of the King of Bavaria, she had dazzled Europe. She didn't dazzle Grass Valley.

"She still retained a slender, graceful figure. She had heavy black hair and the most brilliant flashing eyes I ever beheld. But ordinarily she was such a slattern that to me she was frankly disgusting. When attired in a low-necked gown as was her usual custom, even her liberal use of powder failed to conceal the fact that she stood much in need of a good application of soap."

- One of Lola's neighbors

One day she found her pet bear dead and suspected her husband of the crime. They had a terrible row and she sent him packing.

Life in Grass Valley was scarcely as exciting for Lola as in Bavaria. But for a while she found diversion in promoting her protege, a neighbor's child in whom she found stage talent. She taught her to sing and dance and toss her curls. Little Lotta Crabtree was seven years old when she made her debut doing an Irish jig at a blacksmith shop in Rough and Ready, to the accompaniment of hammer on anvil. Later, Lotta's mother dressed her in an Irish costume, and Lotta danced for the miners in Grass Valley. Since most of the miners were Irish, her vigorous Irish jig was deemed nothing short of sensational, and the stage was covered with gold coins as an honorarium. Lotta Crabtree's career had begun.

Whether Lola's training helped or not, Lotta, vivacious and merry, with red-gold hair and a carefree laugh, went on to become the toast of theater audiences for half a century.

But long before that happened, Lola had wearied of Grass Valley. And Grass Valley had wearied of Lola - the beautiful, the wayward.

She packed up her velvet gowns, cleared out the champagne in the cellar, and left for Australia.

GRASS VALLEY TODAY

Grass Valley is a mixture of century-old buildings and the shiny trappings of modern commerce. The big mines were still going strong as late as the 1950s, employing thousands.

At the end of Mill Street, in Boston Ravine, there's one of the best displays of mining equipment in the gold country. It's the Nevada County Historical Mining Museum, on the ground of the North Star mine. Inside there's a collection of paraphernalia like miners' carbide lamps, mercury flasks, bullion molds. Outside there's a huge Pelton waterwheel, 30 feet in diameter and weighing ten tons.

Up in the pines on the outskirts of town there's another mine, the Empire - one of the oldest and richest gold mines in California and one of the deepest (9,000 feet) in the world. Included in the 770-acre park are the grounds, offices and shops of the mine, along with the stately brick Bourne Mansion, former residence of the mine owner. Framing the two-story stone structure is a 13-acre garden which has been restored as it was when the Bournes spent their summers there.

As is often the case in old Gold Rush towns, it's the hotel that retains the elegance that once was. In Grass Valley, the Holbrooke has the honors.

But the structure that piques everyone's curiousity is the cottage at the corner of Mill and Walsh streets where the scandalous Lola shocked the populace with her outrageous behavior. The house isn't quite the same as when Lola lived there; but with a little imagination, it's possible to picture her at the doorway in her low-cut gown, greeting violinist Ole Bull, or theatrical friends from around the world. She died broken and a bit mad a few years later, in New York.

POSTSCRIPT TO GOLD

The 1852 census revealed that an estimated 12,000 Californians were farming -- that in a state where three years earlier men had died of scurvy for lack of fresh food.

Three years later the state was exporting grain and potatoes.

There was a dramatic increase in the parasol-and-petticoat population; gambling houses closed, churches opened.

The enchantment of California had captivated many, who found their old life far less exciting. They gathered up their families and came back. California had become "home."

But there were also those who couldn't give up their dreams; for them, the gold rush was the epic of their lives. They went on to new gold rushes -- in Oregon, in Nevada, in Alaska.

Those who did return to their old hometowns generally went by ship, for they had seen the misery of the overland trails. For the most part, they looked back with fondness on their experiences. They lovingly preserved their miners' garb as mementoes of their great adventure. And their stories, true or fanciful, became a legacy of a courageous quest for generations yet to come.

It was a wondrous end of a wild quest.

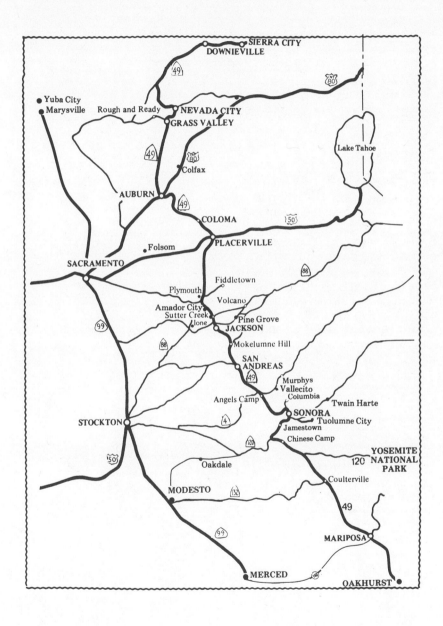

DIRECTORY FOR GOLD COUNTRY INFORMATION

AMADOR COUNTY
Chamber of Commerce
30 S. Hwy. 49 & 88
Box 596, Jackson, CA 95642
Phone: 209-223-0350

County Museum
109 Court St., Jackson, CA 95642
Phone: 209-223-6386

For Gold Information:
Roaring Camp
Box 278, Pine Grove, CA 95665
Phone: 209-296-4100

CALAVERAS COUNTY
Chamber of Commerce
& City of Angels Museum
753 S. Main St.
Box 111, Angels Camp, CA 95222
Phone: 209-736-4444

County Museum & Archives
30 N. Main, P.O. Box 1281
San Andreas, CA 95249
Phone: 209-754-4204

Murphys Old Time Museum
Main St.
Box 94, Murphys, CA 95247

EL DORADO COUNTY
Gold Discovery State Historical Park
Hwy. 49, P.O. Box 265
Coloma, CA 95613
Phone: 916-622-3470

Chamber of Commerce
542 Main St., Placerville, CA 95667
Phone: 916-626-2344

Cameron Park/Shingle Springs
Chamber of Commerce
P.O. Box 341, Shingle Springs, CA 95682
Phone: 916-677-8000

Pollock Pines Chamber of Commerce
P.O. Box 95, Pollock Pines, CA 95726
Phone: 916-644-3970

MADERA COUNTY
Eastern Madera Chamber of Commerce
49074 Civic Circle
Box 369, Oakhurst CA 93644
Phone: 209-683-7766

MARIPOSA COUNTY
Chamber of Commerce
Hwy. 140 & 49 South
Box 425, Mariposa, CA 95338

Museum & History Center
Jessie St. & Hwy. 140
Box 606, Mariposa, CA 95338
Phone: 209-966-2924

No. Mariposa Co. History Center
Corner Hwy. 49 & 132
Box 149, Coulterville, CA 95311
Phone: 209-878-3015

NEVADA COUNTY
County & Grass Valley
Chamber of Commerce
248 Mill St., Grass Valley, CA 95945
Phone: 916-273-4667

Nevada City Chamber of Commerce
130 Main St., Nevada City, CA 95959
Phone: 916-265-2692

Empire Mine State Park
10787 E. Empire St.
Grass Valley, CA 95945
Phone: 916-273-8522

Nevada County Historical Society
Firehouse #1 Museum
Box 1300, Nevada City, CA 95959
Phone: 916-273-7928

Malakoff Diggins State Park
24579 N. Bloomfield-Graniteville Rd.
Box 145, Nevada City, CA 95959
Phone: 916-265-2740

PLACER COUNTY
Visitors Information Center
661 Newcastle Rd., I-80 at Newcastle
Box 749, Newcastle, CA 95658
Phone: 916-885-5616

Placer County Museum
1273 High St., Auburn, CA 95603
Phone: 916-885-9570

Auburn Area Chamber of Commerce
110 High St., Auburn, CA 95603
Phone: 916-885-5616

For Gold Information:
The Metal Smythe
111 Sacramento St.,
Old Auburn, CA 95603
Phone: 916-823-9776

SIERRA COUNTY
Historical Park & Museum
Box 260, Sierra City, CA 96125
Phone: 916-862-1310

TUOLUMNE COUNTY
Columbia State Historical Park
Ranger Office, Main St.
Box 151, Columbia, CA 95310
Phone: 209-532-4301

Chamber of Commerce
31 N. Washington St.
Box 277, Sonora, CA 95370
Phone: 209-532-4212

Tuolumne County Museum
158 W. Bradford Ave.,
Sonora, CA 95370
Phone: 209-532-1317

For Gold Information:
Mother Lode Gold Prospecting
18172 Main St.
Box 974, Jamestown, CA 95327
Phone: 209-984-4653

NOTES

NOTES